TED HUGHES

Poetry in the Making

An Anthology of Poems and
Programmes from
"Listening and Writing"

faber and faber

LONDON · BOSTON

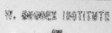

First published in 1967
by Faber and Faber Limited
3 Queen Square London WC1N 3AU
First published in this edition in 1969
Reprinted 1970, 1973, 1975, 1978, 1982 and 1986

Printed in Great Britain by
Whitstable Litho Ltd., Whitstable, Kent

ISBN 0 571 09076 1 (Faber Paperbacks)

To
Pauline Mayne
and
John Edward Fisher

CONTENTS

CONTENTS

ACKNOWLEDGEMENTS

We should like to express our thanks to the following for permission to reproduce poems and a prose extract: Olwyn Hughes for *The Small Box*, *The Donkey*, *Starry Snail* and *The Story of a Story* by Vasco Popa and *You're* by Sylvia Plath from *Ariel* (Faber); Penguin Books Ltd for *The Fly* by Miroslav Holub; The Hogarth Press Ltd for *The Hawk* by George Mackey Brown from *The Year of the Whale*; Chatto & Windus Ltd for *The Fish* by Elizabeth Bishop from *Poems* (1956); Doubleday & Company, Inc. for *Elegy* and *The Storm* by Theodore Roethke, copyright 1961 by Beatrice Roethke as Administratrix of the Estate of Theodore Roethke, from *The Collected Poems of Theodore Roethke*; The Belknap Press of Harvard University Press, Cambridge, Mass. for *Like Rain it Sounded* and *There Came a Wind Like a Bugle* by Emily Dickinson from *The Poems of Emily Dickinson*, Edited by Thomas H. Johnson, copyright 1951, 1955, by The President and Fellows of Harvard College; Routledge & Kegan Paul Ltd for *Mists* and *Teledreamy* by Peter Redgrove from *The Nature of Cold Weather* and *At the White Monument* respectively; Oxford University Press for *Winter Piece* by Charles Tomlinson from *A Peopled Landscape*; A. M. Heath & Company Ltd for an extract from the short story *Powerhouse* by Eudora Welty from *A Curtain of Green* (Penguin Books Ltd); Indiana University Press for *Dirge* by Kenneth Fearing from *New and Collected Poems*; Laurence Pollinger Ltd and the Estate of the late Mrs. Frieda Lawrence for *Bare Almond Trees* and *Mosquito* by D. H. Lawrence from *The Complete Poems of D. H. Lawrence* (Heinemann Ltd); George MacBeth for his poem *Owl*.

INTRODUCTION

In this book I have collected together programmes I wrote at the invitation of Miss Moira Doolan of the BBC Schools Broadcasting Department, for the series *Listening And Writing*. The final piece, *Words and Experience*, was written for the series entitled, *Religion In Its Contemporary Context*. Nothing has been changed, except for the odd word, but a small group of poems, supplementary to those quoted in the programmes, has been added, and also a few suggestions which I hope will help teachers to turn the programmes to immediate classroom use.

The idea behind the first of these programmes, "Capturing Animals", was that I, as a practising writer of verse, should talk about writing in general and my own in particular in a way that might spur my audience—aged between ten and fourteen—to more purposeful efforts in their own writing. I was aware of the dangers, both to me and indirectly to my audience, of assuming a role of this sort, and in the subsequent talks I became deliberately more impersonal. Nevertheless, that first autobiographical setting of my course does continue more or less throughout the book, and it explains several things, such as the emphasis on my own work, which would otherwise have no justification.

I share the general ideas of my generation, and much of what I say is already the practice of many English teachers. The few simple principles of imaginative writing which I collect here are the ones I have found in one way or another especially useful. I keep the talks in their original form in order to keep what could well be the most essential thing in them—the tone and atmosphere which derive from my basic assumption. This assumption is not so common and may even be false, but it is fruitful, so long as one operates within it flexibly and in a practical way. In these talks, I assume that the latent talent for self-expression in any child is immeasurable. As I say, this is very likely false, and even if it were true no teacher could arrange for the psychological crises and the long disciplines that awaken genius in an otherwise ordinary mind. But by showing to a pupil's imagination many opportunities and few restraints, and instilling into him confidence and a natural motive for writing, the odds are that something—maybe not much, but something—of our common genius will begin to put a word in.

The examples I quote and append are meant to serve as models for the kind of writing children can do without becoming false to themselves. As a judge of the *Daily Mirror* Children's Literary Competition for the last three years, I have had plenty of opportunity to confirm or modify my ideas about this. Reading Milton or Keats to children is one thing. Asking them, or allowing them, to use such as models for their own writing is another. All falsities in writing—and the consequent dry-rot that spreads into the whole fabric—come from the notion that there is a stylistic ideal which exists in the abstract, like a special language, to which all men might attain. But teachers of written English should have nothing to do with that, which belongs rather to the study of manners and group jargon. Their words should be not "How to write" but "How to try to say what you really mean"—which is part of the search for self-knowledge and perhaps, in one form or another, grace. So in my examples I have avoided specimens whose great and celebrated charms or powers or both are beyond the sympathy of children. I debated whether to include Dylan Thomas's *Poem In October* which seems to me a unique and beautiful poem, and which looks as though it ought to interest children, but I decided against it finally as being much too sophisticated for my purpose. I have stuck to poems where the language is basically plain, modern speech, and the mental operation simple or very simplified—as in description or fable. At the same time, there will be inevitably more artistic and intellectual and psychological complexity in these works than any child will ever exhaust.

The talks were meant for children, and together with the poems are still for children, though in so far as they are the notes of a provisional teacher, they are also for teachers. Specifically for the teacher, I have added a few notes to Chapters one, two, three, four and five, where I enlarge somewhat on the classroom possibilities of the chapter material. So this book can be used—much as it was in the programmes —as a text and anthology for the class, or as a general handbook for the teacher. Either way, I hope it will be justified.

The Small Box

The small box gets its first teeth
And its small length
Its small width and small emptiness
And all that it has got

The small box is growing bigger
And now the cupboard is in it
That it was in before

And it grows bigger and bigger and bigger
And now has in it the room
And the house and the town and the land
And the world it was in before

The small box remembers its childhood
And by overgreat longing
It becomes a small box again

Now in the small box
Is the whole world quite tiny
You can easily put it in a pocket
Easily steal it easily lose it

Take care of the small box

VASCO POPA

CHAPTER ONE

Capturing Animals

There are all sorts of ways of capturing animals and birds and fish. I spent most of my time, up to the age of fifteen or so, trying out many of these ways and when my enthusiasm began to wane, as it did gradually, I started to write poems.

You might not think that these two interests, capturing animals and writing poems, have much in common. But the more I think back the more sure I am that with me the two interests have been one interest. My pursuit of mice at threshing time when I was a boy, snatching them from under the sheaves as the sheaves were lifted away out of the stack and popping them into my pocket till I had thirty or forty crawling around in the lining of my coat, that and my present pursuit of poems seem to me to be different stages of the same fever. In a way, I suppose, I think of poems as a sort of animal. They have their own life, like animals, by which I mean that they seem quite separate from any person, even from their author, and nothing can be added to them or taken away without maiming and perhaps even killing them. And they have a certain wisdom. They know something special . . . something perhaps which we are very curious to learn. Maybe my concern has been to capture not animals particularly and not poems, but simply things which have a vivid life of their own, outside mine. However all that may be, my interest in animals began when I began. My memory goes back pretty clearly to my third year, and by then I had so many of the toy lead animals you could buy in shops that they went right round our flat-topped fender, nose to tail, with some over.

I had a gift for modelling and drawing, so when I discovered plasticine my zoo became infinite, and when an aunt bought me a thick green-backed animal book for my fourth birthday I began to draw the glossy photographs. The animals looked good in the photographs, but they looked even better in my drawings and were mine. I can remember very vividly the excitement with which I used to sit staring at my drawings, and it is a similar thing I feel nowadays with poems.

My zoo was not entirely an indoors affair. At that time we lived in a valley in the Pennines in West Yorkshire. My brother, who probably had more to do with this passion of mine than anyone else, was a good bit older than I was, and his one interest in life was creeping about on the hillsides with a rifle. He took me along as a retriever and I had to scramble into all kinds of places collecting magpies and owls and rabbits and weasels and rats and curlews that he shot. He could not shoot enough for me. At the same time I used to be fishing daily in the canal, with the long-handled wire-rimmed curtain mesh sort of net.

All that was only the beginning. When I was about eight, we moved to an industrial town in south Yorkshire. Our cat went upstairs and moped in my bedroom for a week, it hated the place so much, and my brother for the same reason left home and became a gamekeeper. But in many ways that move of ours was the best thing that ever happened to me. I soon discovered a farm in the nearby country that supplied all my needs, and soon after, a private estate, with woods and lakes.

My friends were town boys, sons of colliers and railwaymen, and with them I led one life, but all the time I was leading this other life on my own in the country. I never mixed the two lives up, except once or twice disastrously. I still have some diaries that I kept in those years: they record nothing but my catches.

Finally, as I have said, at about fifteen my life grew more complicated and my attitude to animals changed. I accused myself of disturbing their lives. I began to look at them, you see, from their own point of view.

16

And about the same time I began to write poems. Not animal poems. It was years before I wrote what you could call an animal poem and several more years before it occurred to me that my writing poems might be partly a continuation of my earlier pursuit. Now I have no doubt. The special kind of excitement, the slightly mesmerized and quite involuntary concentration with which you make out the stirrings of a new poem in your mind, then the outline, the mass and colour and clean final form of it, the unique living reality of it in the midst of the general lifelessness, all that is too familiar to mistake. This is hunting and the poem is a new species of creature, a new specimen of the life outside your own.

I have now told you very briefly what I believe to be the origins and growth of my interest in writing poetry. I have simplified everything a great deal, but on the whole that is the story. Some of it may seem a bit obscure to you. How can a poem, for instance, about a walk in the rain, be like an animal? Well, perhaps it cannot look much like a giraffe or an emu or an octopus, or anything you might find in a menagerie. It is better to call it an assembly of living parts moved by a single spirit. The living parts are the words, the images, the rhythms. The spirit is the life which inhabits them when they all work together. It is impossible to say which comes first, parts or spirit. But if any of the parts are dead . . . if any of the words, or images or rhythms do not jump to life as you read them . . . then the creature is going to be maimed and the spirit sickly. So, as a poet, you have to make sure that all those parts over which you have control, the words and rhythms and images, are alive. That is where the difficulties begin. Yet the rules, to begin with, are very simple. Words that live are those which we hear, like "click" or "chuckle", or which we see, like "freckled" or "veined", or which we taste, like "vinegar" or "sugar", or touch, like "prickle" or "oily", or smell, like "tar" or "onion". Words which belong directly to one of the five senses. Or words which act and seem to use their muscles, like "flick" or "balance".

But immediately things become more difficult. "Click" not only gives you a sound, it gives you the notion of a sharp movement . . . such as your tongue makes in saying "click". It also gives you the feel of something light and brittle, like a snapping twig. Heavy things do not click, nor do soft bendable ones. In the same way, tar not only smells strongly. It is sticky to touch, with a particular thick and choking stickiness. Also it moves, when it is soft, like a black snake, and has a beautiful black gloss. So it is with most words. They belong to several of the senses at once, as if each one had eyes, ears and tongue, or ears and fingers and a body to move with. It is this little goblin in a word which is its life and its poetry, and it is this goblin which the poet has to have under control.

Well, you will say, this is hopeless. How do you control all that. When the words are pouring out how can you be sure that you do not have one of these side meanings of the word "feathers" getting all stuck up with one of the side meanings of the word "treacle", a few words later. In bad poetry this is exactly what happens, the words kill each other. Luckily, you do not have to bother about it so long as you do one thing.

That one thing is, imagine what you are writing about. See it and live it. Do not think it up laboriously, as if you were working out mental arithmetic. Just look at it, touch it, smell it, listen to it, turn yourself into it. When you do this, the words look after themselves, like magic. If you do this you do not have to bother about commas or full-stops or that sort of thing. You do not look at the words either. You keep your eyes, your ears, your nose, your taste, your touch, your whole being on the thing you are turning into words. The minute you flinch, and take your mind off this thing, and begin to look at the words and worry about them . . . then your worry goes into them and they set about killing each other. So you keep going as long as you can, then look back and see what you have written. After a bit of practice, and after telling yourself a few times that you do not care how other people have written about this thing, this is the way you find it; and after telling yourself you are going to use any old word that comes into your head so long as it seems right at the moment of writing it down, you will surprise yourself. You will read back through what you have written and you will get a shock. You will have captured a spirit, a creature.

After all that, I ought to give you some examples and show you some of my own more recently acquired specimens.

An animal I never succeeded in keeping alive is the fox. I was always frustrated: twice by a farmer, who killed cubs I had caught before I could get to them, and once by a poultry keeper who freed my cub while his dog waited. Years after those events I was sitting up late one snowy night in dreary lodgings in London. I had written nothing for a year or so but that night I got the idea I might write something and I wrote in a few minutes the following poem: the first "animal" poem I ever wrote. Here it is—*The Thought-Fox*.

> I imagine this midnight moment's forest:
> Something else is alive
> Beside the clock's loneliness
> And this blank page where my fingers move,
>
> Through the window I see no star:
> Something more near
> Though deeper within darkness
> Is entering the loneliness:
>
> Cold, delicately as the dark snow,
> A fox's nose touches twig, leaf;
> Two eyes serve a movement, that now
> And again now, and now, and now
>
> Sets neat prints into the snow
> Between trees, and warily a lame
> Shadow lags by stump and in hollow
> Of a body that is bold to come

Across clearings, an eye,
A widening deepening greenness,
Brilliantly, concentratedly,
Coming about its own business

Till, with a sudden sharp hot stink of fox
It enters the dark hole of the head.
The window is starless still; the clock ticks,
The page is printed.

This poem does not have anything you could easily call a meaning. It is about a fox, obviously enough, but a fox that is both a fox and not a fox. What sort of a fox is it that can step right into my head where presumably it still sits . . . smiling to itself when the dogs bark. It is both a fox and a spirit. It is a real fox; as I read the poem I see it move, I see it setting its prints, I see its shadow going over the irregular surface of the snow. The words show me all this, bringing it nearer and nearer. It is very real to me. The words have made a body for it and given it somewhere to walk.

If, at the time of writing this poem, I had found livelier words, words that could give me much more vividly its movements, the twitch and craning of its ears, the slight tremor of its hanging tongue and its breath making little clouds, its teeth bared in the cold, the snow-crumbs dropping from its pads as it lifts each one in turn, if I could have got the words for all this, the fox would probably be even more real and alive to me now, than it is as I read the poem. Still, it is there as it is. If I had not caught the real fox there in the words I would never have saved the poem. I would have thrown it into the wastepaper basket as I have thrown so many other hunts that did not get what I was after. As it is, every time I read the poem the fox comes up again out of the darkness and steps into my head. And I suppose that long after I am gone, as long as a copy of the poem exists, every time anyone reads it the fox will get up somewhere out in the darkness and come walking towards them.

So, you see, in some ways my fox is better than an ordinary fox. It will live for ever, it will never suffer from hunger or hounds. I have it with me wherever I go. And I made it. And all through imagining it clearly enough and finding the living words.

Here, in this next poem, is one of my prize catches. I used to be a very keen angler for pike, as I still am when I get the chance, and I did most of my early fishing in a quite small lake, really a large pond. This pond went down to a great depth in one place. Sometimes, on hot days, we would see something like a railway sleeper lying near the surface, and there certainly were huge pike in that pond. I suppose they are even bigger by now. Recently I felt like doing some pike fishing, but in circumstances where there was no chance of it, and over the days, as I remembered the extreme pleasures of that sport, bits of the following poem began to arrive. As you will see, by looking at the place in my memory very hard and very carefully and by using the words that grew naturally out of the pictures and feelings, I captured not just a pike, I captured the whole pond, including the monsters I never even hooked. Here is the poem which I called *Pike*.

Pike, three inches long, perfect
Pike in all parts, green tigering the gold.
Killers from the egg: the malevolent aged grin.
They dance on the surface among the flies.

Or move, stunned by their own grandeur,
Over a bed of emerald, silhouette
Of submarine delicacy and horror.
A hundred feet long in their world.

In ponds, under the heat-struck lily pads—
Gloom of their stillness:
Logged on last year's black leaves, watching upwards.
Or hung in an amber cavern of weeds.

The jaws' hooked clamp and fangs
Not to be changed at this date;
A life subdued to its instrument;
The gills kneading quietly, and the pectorals.

Three we kept behind glass,
Jungled in weed: three inches, four,
And four and a half: fed fry to them—
Suddenly there were two. Finally one

With a sag belly and the grin it was born with.
And indeed they spare nobody.
Two, six pounds each, over two feet long,
High and dry and dead in the willow-herb—

One jammed past its gills down the other's gullet:
The outside eye stared: as a vice locks—
The same iron in this eye
Though its film shrank in death.

A pond I fished, fifty yards across,
Whose lilies and muscular tench
Had outlasted every visible stone
Of the monastery that planted them—

Stilled legendary depth:
It was as deep as England. It held
Pike too immense to stir, so immense and old
That past nightfall I dared not cast

But silently cast and fished
With the hair frozen on my head
For what might move, for what eye might move.
The still splashes on the dark pond,

Owls hushing the floating woods
Frail on my ear against the dream
Darkness beneath night's darkness had freed,
That rose slowly towards me, watching.

* * * *

Note

"Animals" are the subject here, but more important is the idea of headlong, concentrated improvisation on a set theme. Once the subject has been chosen, the exercise should be given a set length, say one side of a page, and a set time limit—ten minutes would be an ideal minimum though in practice it obviously varies a good deal to suit the class. These artificial limits create a crisis, which rouses the brain's resources: the compulsion towards haste overthrows the ordinary precautions, flings everything into top gear, and many things that are usually hidden find themselves rushed into the open. Barriers break down, prisoners come out of their cells.

Another artificial help is to give each phrase a fresh line. The result should be a free poem of sorts where grammar, sentence structure etc, are all sacrificed in an attempt to break fresh and accurate perceptions and words out of the reality of the subject chosen.

As in training dogs, these exercises should be judged by their successes, not their mistakes or shortcomings. Wherever a teacher can recognize and appreciate a hit, a moment of truth, it is a very poor pupil that does not soon get the idea.

In my experience, it is a help to give the pupils some time to carry the subject in their heads before they begin to write. I have always thought it would be productive to give out at the beginning of term some of the subjects that are going to be written about during the next weeks. The pupils would then watch the intervening lessons more purposefully, and we cannot prevent ourselves from preparing for a demand that we know is going to be made. Then when the time comes to write, it should be regarded as a hundred-yards' dash.

In this, as in all the exercises that follow, the chief aim should be to develop the habit of all-out flowing exertion, for a short, concentrated period, in a definite direction.

23

Badger

When midnight comes a host of dogs and men
Go out and track the badger to his den,
And put a sack within his hole, and lie
Till the old grunting badger passes by.
He comes and hears—they let the strongest loose.
The old fox hears the noise and drops the goose.
The poacher shoots and hurries from the cry,
And the old hare half wounded buzzes by.
They get a forked stick to bear him down
And clap the dogs and take him to the town,
And bait him all the day with many dogs,
And laugh and shout and fright the scampering hogs.
He runs along and bites at all he meets:
They shout and hollo down the noisy streets.

He turns about to face the loud uproar
And drives the rebels to their very door.
The frequent stone is hurled where'er they go;
When badgers fight, then everyone's a foe.
The dogs are clapt and urged to join the fray;
The badger turns and drives them all away.
Though scarcely half as big, demure and small,
He fights with dogs for hours and beats them all.
The heavy mastiff, savage in the fray,
Lies down and licks his feet and turns away.
The bulldog knows his match and waxes cold,
The badger grins and never leaves his hold.
He drives the crowd and follows at their heels
And bites them through—the drunkard swears and reels.

The frighted women take the boys away,
The blackguard laughs and hurries on the fray.
He tries to reach the woods, an awkward race,
But sticks and cudgels quickly stop the chase.
He turns again and drives the noisy crowd
And beats the many dogs in noises loud.

He drives away and beats them every one,
And then they loose them all and set them on.
He falls as dead and kicked by boys and men,
Then starts and grins and drives the crowd again;
Till kicked and torn and beaten out he lies
And leaves his hold, and cackles, groans, and dies.

JOHN CLARE

The Fly

She sat on a willow trunk
watching
part of the battle of Crecy,
the shouts,
the gasps,
the groans,
The trampling and the tumbling.

During the fourteenth charge
of the French cavalry
she mated
with a brown-eyed male fly
from Vadincourt.

She rubbed her legs together
as she sat on the disembowelled horse
meditating
on the immortality of flies.

With relief she alighted
on the blue tongue
of the Duke of Clervaux.

When silence settled
and only the whisper of decay
softly circled the bodies

and only
a few arms and legs
still twitched jerkily under the trees

she began to lay her eggs
on the single eye
of Johann Uhr,
the Royal Armourer.

And thus it was
that she was eaten by a swift
fleeing
From the fires of Estrées.

MIROSLAV HOLUB
(translated by Ian Milner & George Theiner)

The Donkey

Sometimes it brays
Bathes itself in dust
Sometimes
And then you notice it

Otherwise
You just see its ears
On the head of a planet
And no sign of it

VASCO POPA
(translated by Anne Pennington)

The Hawk

On Sunday the hawk fell on Bigging
And a chicken screamed

Lost in its own little snowstorm.
And on Monday he fell on the moor
  And the Field Club
  Raised a hundred silent prisms.
And on Tuesday he fell on the hill
  And the happy lamb
  Never knew why the loud collie straddled him.
And on Wednesday he fell on a bush
  And the blackbird
  Laid by his little flute for the last time.
And on Thursday he fell on Cleat
  And peerie Tom's rabbit
  Swung in a single arc from shore to hill.
And on Friday he fell on a ditch
  But the rampant rat,
  That eye and that tooth, quenched his flame.
And on Saturday he fell on Bigging
  And Jock lowered his gun
  And nailed a small wing over the corn.

GEORGE MACKAY BROWN

The Fish

I caught a tremendous fish
and held him beside the boat
half out of water, with my hook
fast in the corner of his mouth.
He didn't fight.
He hadn't fought at all.
He hung a grunting weight,
battered and venerable
and homely. Here and there
his brown skin hung in strips
like ancient wall-paper,
and its pattern of darker brown

27

was like wall-paper:
shapes like full-blown roses
stained and lost through age.
He was speckled with barnacles,
fine rosettes of lime,
and infested
with tiny white sea-lice,
and underneath two or three
rags of green weed hung down.
While his gills were breathing in
the terrible oxygen
—the frightening gills
fresh and crisp with blood,
that can cut so badly—
I thought of the coarse white flesh
packed in like feathers,
the big bones and the little bones,
the dramatic reds and blacks
of his shiny entrails,
and the pink swim-bladder
like a big peony.
I looked into his eyes
which were far larger than mine
but shallower, and yellowed,
the irises backed and packed
with tarnished tinfoil
seen through the lenses
of old scratched isinglass.
They shifted a little, but not
to return my stare.
—It was more like the tipping
of an object toward the light.
I admired his sullen face,
the mechanism of his jaw,
and then I saw
that from his lower lip
—if you could call it a lip—
grim, wet and weapon-like,
hung five old pieces of fish-line,

or four and a wire leader
with the swivel still attached,
with all their five big hooks
grown firmly in his mouth.
A green line, frayed at the end
where he broke it, two heavier lines,
and a fine black thread
still crimped from the strain and snap
when it broke and he got away.
Like medals with their ribbons
frayed and wavering
a five-haired beard of wisdom
trailing from his aching jaw.
I stared and stared
and victory filled up
the little rented boat,
from the pool of bilge
where oil had spread a rainbow
around the rusted engine,
to the bailer rusted orange,
the sun-cracked thwarts,
the oarlocks on their strings,
the gunnels—until everything
was rainbow, rainbow, rainbow!
And I let the fish go.

ELIZABETH BISHOP

Starry Snail

You crept out after the rain
After the starry rain

The stars have built a small house for you
By themselves out of your bones
Where are you taking it on that towel

Time goes limping after you
To catch you up to trample you
Put out your horns snail

You slide over the vast countenance
Which you will never be able to see
Straight to the jaws of the good-for-nothing

Turn on to the life-line
Of my dreaming palm
Before it is too late

And leave me as a legacy
The miraculous towel of silver

VASCO POPA
(translated by Anne Pennington)

The Marvel

A baron of the sea, the great tropic
swordfish, spreadeagled on the thirsty deck
where sailors killed him, in the bright Pacific,

yielded to the sharp enquiring blade
the eye which guided him and found his prey
in the dim place where he was lord.

Which is an instrument forged in semi-darkness;
yet taken from the corpse of this strong traveller
becomes a powerful enlarging glass

reflecting the unusual sun's heat.
With it a sailor writes on the hot wood
the name of a harlot in his last port.

For it is one most curious device
of many, kept by the interesting waves,
for I suppose the querulous soft voice

of mariners who rotted into ghosts
digested by the gluttonous tides
could recount many. Let them be your hosts

and take you where their forgotten ships lie
with fishes going over the tall masts—
all this emerges from the burning eye.

And to engrave that word the sun goes through
with the power of the sea
writing her name and a marvel too.

KEITH DOUGLAS

CHAPTER TWO

Wind and Weather

Have you noticed how your mood depends on the weather? All living things are natural barometers, and change as the weather changes. Every fisherman knows that fish, for instance, behave differently from minute to minute according to the weather, and some painstaking fishermen get to know just how any particular change of weather will affect certain fish. No doubt some of you know how furiously active and ravenous eels become, and how persistent in biting flies become, in the heavy minutes before a thunderstorm breaks. One reason for our responding in this way, is that changes in air pressure and atmospheric electricity directly affect the chemical processes of our bodies, and we experience these changes in our bodily chemistry as changes in our feelings. If you imagine your conscious mind as the speaker of a radio, and your body as the inside works and the valves—then the weather is something that fiddles with the control knobs.

What has all this talk about the weather to do with poetry? This. Poetry is not made out of thoughts or casual fancies. It is made out of experiences which change our bodies, and spirits, whether momentarily or for good. There are plenty of different experiences which do this, and there is no drawing a line at what the limit is. The sight of a certain word can so affect you that delicate instruments can easily detect the changes in your skin perspiration, the rate of your pulse and so on, just as surely as when the sight of an apple makes your mouth water or your sudden fear in an empty house makes you chill. The work of most good poets is written out of some especially affecting and individual experience which they have

32

undergone at some time, or perhaps which, because of something in their nature, keeps happening to them again and again. The wider this experience is, the more of ordinary life it includes, the greater the poet, as a rule. But some very great poets have written out of quite a limited and peculiar experience. Wordsworth's greatest poetry seems to be rooted in two or three rather similar experiences he had as a boy among the Cumberland mountains.

Fortunately, as I say, we do not have to have had an extraordinary experience, like his, to be able to produce some sort of poetry. And one poetic experience which all of us go through, whether we like it or not, is the hour by hour effect on us of the weather. Out of this almost everybody, at some time in their lives, can produce pieces of poetry. Perhaps not very great poetry, but still, poetry they are glad to have written. One of the most striking features of weather is the wind. The wind, in all its phases, coming, here, going and gone, might be said to be one of the great subjects of poetry. Almost every poet, when he mentions the wind, touches one of his good moments of poetry. Why poets should be so interested in the wind, or the absence of it, is a bit of a mystery. Perhaps it represents simply inspiration. The Old Testament prophets were often carried off to their visions in a great wind, or heard extraordinary things out of unnatural stillness. A strong wind certainly stirs your mind up, as if it actually could enter your head, and sometimes on such occasions you get the feeling of having lost your bearings, and that something terrible is about to happen, almost as if it were the beginning of an earthquake.

On and off I live in a house on top of a hill in the Pennines, where the wind blows without obstruction across the tops of the moors. I have experienced some gales in that house, and here is a poem I once wrote about one of them. The grass of the fields there is of a particularly brilliant watered green, and the stone walls of the enclosures that cover the hillsides like a great net thrown over whales, look coal black. The poem is called simply: *Wind*.

This house has been far out at sea all night,
The woods crashing through darkness, the booming hills,
Wind stampeding the fields under the windows
Floundering black astride and blinding wet

Till day rose. Then, under an orange sky,
The hills had new places, and wind wielded
Blade-light, luminous black and emerald
Flexing like the lens of a mad eye.

At noon I scaled along the house-side as far as
The coal-house door. I dared once to look up:
Through the brunt wind that dented the balls of my eyes
The tent of the hills drummed and strained its guy-rope,

The fields quivering, the skyline a grimace,
At any second to bang and vanish with a flap:
The wind flung a magpie away, and a black
Back gull bent like an iron bar slowly. The house

Rang like some fine green goblet in the note
That any second would shatter it. Now deep
In chairs, in front of the great fire, we grip
Our hearts and cannot entertain book, thought,

Or each other. We watch the fire blazing,
And feel the roots of the house move, but sit on,
Seeing the window tremble to come in,
Hearing the stones cry out under the horizons.

In writing that poem I was mainly concerned with the
strength of the blast, the way it seems to shake the world up
like a box of toys.

In this next poem, the American poet Theodore Roethke
concentrates on the step by step rising of a storm. You will
notice how he expresses the fear and dread that he and his wife
feel, not by telling us that they are frightened, but by describing all the small frightening details which he observes, as if he
were making notes for a film of the occasion. You know how

ominous, in a film, is a sudden close-up of a blowing piece of paper, then a loosely banging door, then a furiously beating tree. Here is the poem, which he calls: *The Storm*. It takes place in an Italian seaside town.

Against the stone breakwater,
Only an ominous lapping,
While the wind whines overhead,
Coming down from the mountain,
Whistling between the arbours, the winding terraces;
A thin whine of wires, a rattling and flapping of leaves,
And the small streetlamp swinging and slamming against the
    lamp-pole.
Where have the people gone?
There is one light on the mountain.
Along the sea-wall a steady sloshing of the swell,
The waves not yet high, but even,
Coming closer and closer upon each other;
A fine fume of rain driving in from the sea,
Riddling the sand, like a wide spray of buckshot,
The wind from the sea and the wind from the mountain con-
    tending,
Flicking the foam from the whitecaps straight upwards into the
    darkness.
A time to go home!
And a child's dirty shift billows upward out of an alley;
A cat runs from the wind as we do,
Between the whitening trees, up Santa Lucia.
Where the heavy door unlocks
And our breath comes more easy.
Then a crack of thunder, and the black rain runs over us, over
The flat-roofed houses, coming down in gusts, beating
The walls, the slatted windows, driving
The last watcher indoors, moving the cardplayers closer
To their cards, their Lachryma Christi.
We creep to our bed and its straw mattress.
We wait, we listen.
The storm lulls off, then redoubles,
Bending the trees halfway down to the ground,

Shaking loose the last wizened oranges in the orchard,
Flattening the limber carnations.
A spider eases himself down from a swaying light bulb,
Running over the coverlet, down under the iron bedstead.
The bulb goes on and off, weakly.
Water roars in the cistern.
We lie closer on the gritty pillow,
Breathing heavily, hoping—
For the great last leap of the wave over the breakwater,
The flat boom on the beach of the towering sea-swell,
The sudden shudder as the jutting sea-cliff collapses
And the hurricane drives the dead straw into the living pine-tree.

That is very simple writing, nothing peculiar or special about it, and you might all keep it in mind when you come to try writing about something similar.

Perhaps the most terrible moment of wind is the first breath of an electrical storm. The great American poetess, Emily Dickinson, has many wonderful poems about various weathers, but here is one of her best. No other poet, to my knowledge, has captured that sinister foreboding of the first eerie gloomy gust just so vividly. The landscape comes alive as if the touch of the wind and the strange light had turned it into nightmare. Notice how every line is special, as if a procession of visions was passing in front of her eyes. The poem has no title.

There came a wind like a bugle—
It quivered through the grass
And a green chill upon the heat
So ominous did pass
We barred the windows and the doors
As from an emerald ghost—
The doom's electric moccasin
That very instant passed—
On a strange mob of panting trees
And fences fled away
And rivers where the houses ran
The living looked that day
The bell within the steeple wild

36

The flying tidings told
How much can come and much can go,
And yet abide the world!

After the wind, it is natural to expect rain. Here is Emily Dickinson again, writing not about a storm but a cloudburst. Notice again how every phrase is a fresh event, as she presents the whole busy scene, step by step. Again, the poem has no title:

Like rain it sounded, till it curved
And then I knew twas wind;
It walked as wet as any wave
And swept as dry as sand.
When it had pushed itself away
To some remotest plain
A coming as of hosts was heard—
That was indeed the rain!
It filled the wells, it pleased the pools,
It warbled in the road,
It pulled the spigot from the hills
And let the floods abroad;
It loosened acres, lifted seas,
The sites of centres stirred,
Then like Elijah rode away
Upon a wheel of cloud.

Unlike the poem by Theodore Roethke, these poems by Emily Dickinson are full of metaphors, but they are not casual similitudes or a way of being vaguely poetic and suggestive. They make her meaning more precise than simple language could, as when she says of the wind, "It walked as wet as any wave/And swept as dry as sand", and in the last lines, where she says of the rainstorm: "Then like Elijah rode away/Upon a wheel of cloud." She conveys all the surrounding brilliance of the heavens after a rainstorm, the broken sky and gaps of new light, the withdrawing, fiercely coloured cloud that brought the rain, the rainbow, and the wide, glistening after-glory over the whole scene. This complicated and huge panorama appears in one flash out of her single surprising image.

A very different kind of rain falls through this next poem, which is by Edward Thomas. This is the soaking, coming and going, day after day kind of rain, which is one of our national prides. His method of describing the rain is more like Theodore Roethke's than Emily Dickinson's. That is, he uses simple language, and takes microscopic visual close-ups of one thing after another, till the scene gradually fits together as we read, and the atmosphere begins to soak into us. The lines move hesitantly, like the rain. The whole mood is gentle and watchful as you might imagine the mood of a tramp who sits in a dry shelter under a hedge, with no desire to move and no need, looking out at this endlessly returning rain. The poem is called: *After Rain*.

> The rain of a night and a day and a night
> Stops at the light
> Of this pale choked day. The peering sun
> Sees what has been done.
> The road under the trees has a border new
> Of purple hue
> Inside the border of bright thin grass:
> For all that has
> Been left by November of leaves is torn
> From hazel and thorn
> And the greater trees. Throughout the copse
> No dead leaf drops
> On grey grass, green moss, burnt-orange fern,
> At the wind's return;
> The leaflets out of the ash-tree shed
> Are thinly spread
> In the road, like little black fish, inlaid
> As if they played.
> What hangs from the myriad branches down there
> So hard and bare
> Is twelve yellow apples lovely to see
> On one crab tree.

And on each twig of every drop in the dell
Uncountable
Crystals both dark and bright of the rain
That begins again.

All the poems I have mentioned so far are saturated in some
particular moment of the weather. Here is a poem about mists,
by Peter Redgrove, that takes a more detached view. He sees
the mist, all its moving forms and gesticulations, as a soft
swarm of almost living things. He is not so interested in the
mood of walking through mists, as he is in their strange nature,
their strange kind of life. He calls the poem: *Mists*.

They do not need the moon for ghostliness
These mists jostling the boles,
These boy-wraiths and ogre-fumes
That hollow to a breasting walk;
They are harmless enough in all conscience,
Wetting eyelashes and growing moulds,
And do not speak at all, unless their walking flood
Is a kind of languid speech. Like ghosts
Dawn filches them for dews.
They wink at me from grasses pushed aside
And impart a high polish to my shoes
That dry in dullness, milky, sloven leather,
From walking in ghostways where tall mists grope.

So far I have chosen poems about very definite sorts of
weather: wind, rain and mist. From these poems I hope you
have picked some hints as to how you might begin to get hold
of your own feelings about the infinitely changeable weather,
and to write poems you will be glad to have written.

*   *   *   *

Note

As with Chapter One, the exercises here will most naturally
take the form of imitations of the pieces quoted. The one thing
to make sure of is that the topic be as definite as possible, and

preferably based on some specific memory. I doubt if much would come of just "snow", as a subject. But there are an infinite number of categories within the general concept "snow", and it is the teacher's job to help the pupil narrow the idea down to a vivid memory or fantasy. To ask a class to suggest all the possible and impressive occasions of "snow" is to evoke some surprisingly special ideas and at the same time rouses the collective spirit of the class, from which each individual, to some extent, draws inspiration.

The actual work of the exercise then follows, as for Chapter One.

Winter-Piece

You wake, all windows blind—embattled sprays
grained on the mediaeval glass.
Gates snap like gunshot
as you handle them. Five-barred fragility
sets flying fifteen rooks who go together
silently ravenous above this winter-piece
that will not feed them. They alight
beyond, scavenging, missing everything
but the bladed atmosphere, the white resistance.
Ruts with iron flanges track
through a hard decay
where you discern once more
oak-leaf by hawthorn, for the frost
rewhets their edges. In a perfect web
blanched along each spoke
and circle of its woven wheel,
the spider hangs, grasp unbroken
and death-masked in cold. Returning
you see the house glint-out behind
its holed and ragged glaze,
frost-fronds all streaming.

CHARLES TOMLINSON

Teledreamy

The weather is television weather, gusty
From the pasty square of light, whirls showering black;
Her fingers go on typing, very lightly.

We wring our eyes in a deluge of shadows—
Snow squalls across the screen—at this
Her father's fingers wriggle in their stains,
Resume their quiet flicker.

I yawn and shadows run in my mouth, crawl up my nose;
Her mother's jigsaw mouth grins and mourns, grins and mourns,
Though her eyes never leave the story,
Then hailstones gallop up the screen
And her parents disappear in dust
Of whirling shadows, emerge,
Resume their quiet flicker.

Mouths brimming with shadows,
I yawn into our quiet flicker;
We advance, retire; advance, retire
In our quiet flicker.

PETER REDGROVE

CHAPTER THREE

Writing About People

For some reason or other, we like to read about other people. We want to know everything about them. In fact, we are very nosy by nature. Much of the effort of writers, ever since words began, has gone into discovering how to bring people alive in words. This is something everybody has to learn for themselves, though of course you can learn a good deal from the example of people who have written before you. Learning from example, however, can be dangerous. You are as likely to learn something that is bad for you as something that is good. I am going to quote a few examples for you, but just look at them very cautiously. Be ready to decide that you would like to see it done otherwise.

Out of all the writing about people that is in existence, it is unbelievable how little seems to contain any life at all. It seems that it must be terribly difficult to write about a person in such a way that the reader can feel what he was like alive, what his presence was. History tends to be boring for just this reason— it does not often contain people. Most history textbooks might be recording events on a planet where no human beings lived, only names, and names did things. History becomes interesting, however, just as soon as we begin to see vividly, and sense the living presence of, the people who created it. Then we begin to imagine how this person looked and felt during these events, and as soon as our imaginations are engaged, the whole thing becomes exciting, and we can learn from it.

From time to time I have read a good deal about Sir Francis Bacon, the great Elizabethan statesman and philosopher. He interested me. But it was some time before he really came alive for me. I read a lot about him while just searching for the clue that would tell me what he was really like. At last I found it. I read that he had peculiar eyes—eyes, we are told, like a viper. Why this particular detail should satisfy me, I do not know, but at once I was able to feel I knew exactly what that man was like. I felt to be in his presence. And everything that I could remember about him became at once near and real. And this is what we want. Whether we are reading a letter that gives an account of a new sister-in-law, or reading about Caesar, we want that person to come near and real, so that we shall know.

The art of choosing just those details about a person which catch his or her life, is not an easy one. As I say, everybody has to learn it afresh. You cannot make a person come alive in your words simply by describing what he looks like in general, saying, for instance, "He had a big nose and was bald, and wore blue mostly, but sometimes brown. I think he had brown eyes." All that tells you nothing: the person described might be a million different people. He might be thin and dwarfish, or immensely fat, and tall. His big nose might be a Roman nose, a spindly knobbly nose, or a hammered-out boxer's nose. From that description, you cannot be sure. Your imagination is not given any definite cue, and so it does not go into action, and the whole art of writing is to make your reader's imagination go into action.

On the other hand, you do not make things any better when you try to fit the picture grain by grain into the reader's imagination, as if you were trying to paint it there carefully, as in:

"His brow, at the height of his eyebrows, was precisely seven and a quarter inches across, and from the lowest root of the hair at the mid-point of the hairline along the upper brow, to the slight horizontal wrinkle in the saddle of his nose, measured three inches exact. His hair was the colour of a rough coconut, parted on the left, closely cropped over the ears and up the back, but perfectly straight, and with no single hair, on any part of his head, more than two and two-thirds inches long...."

And so on. To describe a man at that rate you would need a whole book, and you would be bored reading the first paragraph. But did anything in that passage strike my imagination? Yes. One thing did. When the man's hair was described as the colour of a rough coconut, I not only saw exactly what colour it was, I even felt its texture, its rough, bristly grain. This comparison set my imagination into action. It is one of those curious facts that when two things are compared in a metaphor or a simile, we see both of them much more distinctly than if they were mentioned separately as having nothing to do with each other. A comparison is like a little puzzle. When I say, "His hair was like a rough coconut's"—you say to yourself, "How can it be?" And this rouses your imagination to supply the answers, showing just how hair can be like coconut hair, without the head beneath being an actual coconut. You are forced to look more closely, and to think, and make distinctions, and be surprised at what you find—and all this adds to the strength and vividness of your final impression. And it all happens in a flash. Just give yourself a few odd similes or metaphors and see how they set your imagination going:

How is a dragonfly like a helicopter?

How is a tramp-steamer in a rough sea like an old man?

How is a ball like an echo?

So, in this business of bringing people to life in words, comparisons can be helpful. Now for an example. In this following poem a girl in a café is described as a white stone on the floor of the sea. The poet does not just say that is what she is like, and no more. He builds the comparison up, piece by piece, so that the whole situation seems to be taking place beneath the sea. The poem is by Keith Douglas, and it is called *Behaviour of Fish in an Egyptian Tea-Garden*:

As a white stone draws down the fish
she on the seafloor of the afternoon
draws down men's glances and their cruel wish
for love. Her red lip on the spoon

slips in a morsel of ice-cream. Her hands
white as a shell, are submarine
fronds sinking with spread fingers, lean
along the table, carmined at the ends.

A cotton magnate, an important fish
with great eyepouches and a golden mouth
through the frail reefs of furniture swims out
and idling, suspended, stays to watch.

A crustacean old man, clamped to his chair
sits near her and might coldly see
her charms through fissures where the eyes should be;
or else his teeth are parted in a stare.

Captain on leave, a lean dark mackerel
lies in the offing, turns himself and looks
through currents of sound. The flat-eyed flatfish
sucks on a straw, staring from its repose, laxly.

And gallants in shoals swim up and lag
circling and passing near the white attraction;
sometimes pausing, opening a conversation:
fish pause so to nibble or tug.

But now the ice-cream is finished, is
paid for. The fish swim off on business
and she sits alone at the table, a white stone
useless except to a collector, a rich man.

This poem is not simply comparing everything to fish and
things undersea. It is not turning everybody into fish. It is
making you see more distinctly than you otherwise might, just
what sort of people they are, and just how they are behaving.
To call a man "A cotton magnate" gives us no idea of what he
is like, it is just a bare fact about his job. But when we are told
that he is

    . . . an important fish
    with great eyepouches and a golden mouth

we see exactly what he is, his bloated saggy face and gold-filled teeth. It is the same with the old man:

> A crustacean old man, clamped to his chair
> sits near her and might coldly see
> her charms through fissures where the eyes should be;
> or else his teeth are parted in a stare.

He seems to be actually there, we can feel him thinking.

Here is another passage, not a poem this time, describing an American Negro jazz pianist preparing for action. What the writer is after here is to catch Powerhouse, as this pianist is called, in the electric moment just before the band starts to play. Just notice how the writer's eye fixes on the vital details —like the movement of the musician's eyebrows, and poise of his finger over the first note.

"Powerhouse is not a show-off like the Harlem boys, not drunk, not crazy—he's in a trance; he's a person of joy, a fanatic. He listens as much as he performs, a look of hideous powerful rapture on his face. Big arched eyebrows that never stop travelling, like a Jew's—wandering-Jew eyebrows. When he plays he beats down the piano and seat and wears them away. He is in motion every moment—what could be more obscene? There is he with his great head, fat stomach, and little round piston legs, and long yellow-sectioned strong big fingers, at rest about the size of bananas. Of course, you know how he sounds—you've heard him on records—but still you need to see him. He's going all the time, like skating around the skating rink or rowing a boat. It makes everybody crowd around, here in his shadowless steel-trussed hall, with the rose-like posters of Nelson Eddy and the testimonial for the mind-reading horse in handwriting magnified five-hundred times. Then all quietly he lays a finger on a key with the promise and serenity of a sybil touching the book . . .

"Powerhouse has as much as possible done by signals. Everybody, laughing as if to hide a weakness, will sooner or later hand up a written request. Powerhouse reads each one, studying with a secret face: that is the face which looks like a mask—anybody's; there is a moment when he makes a decision. Then a light slides under his eyelids and he says: '92!' or some combination of figures, never a name. Before a number the band is all frantic, misbehaving, pushing, like children in a schoolroom and he is a teacher getting silence. His hands over the keys he says sternly: 'You-all ready? You-all ready to do some serious walking?'—waits—then, STAMP. Quiet. STAMP, for the second time. This is absolute. Then a set of rhythmic kicks against the floor to communicate the tempo. Then O Lord! say the distended eyes from beyond the boundary of the trumpets, hello and goodbye, and they are all down the first note like a waterfall."

That is a character in action, and it is a complicated action, one you would imagine pretty difficult to describe. But the writer here seems to find it easy and natural enough, it sounds almost like talk. The description depends, you see, on the details—the most interesting details, the details that catch your interest, the details you remember—then it is just a matter of presenting those vividly in words. And that is the whole difficulty of presenting a character vividly: what are the interesting details about him? What is it about him or her that catches your eye?

Both these pieces, about the girl and about Powerhouse, describe a character at a definite time and in a definite place, doing a definite thing. How is it different when we want to set forth, briefly, a person's entire life, or to give an impression of what he or she was like in general?

If you were asked to set down an account of your father, in twenty lines, how would you do it? You would describe the actions and doings that seem most characteristic of him, that distinguish him from everybody else. You would not be likely to say he goes to work every day, because that is taken for granted. But you might mention that he is a champion dart-thrower, if he is, or that he is always sitting cracking his

47

knuckles, or that he has a pickle-tooth. In gossip and ordinary conversation everybody selects just such details naturally. When you are describing somebody to your friend, you do not describe their hair, their eyes, their clothes, etc., unless there is something unique about those things. If they have one eye blue and one eye green, for instance, it would probably be the first thing you would mention. But if they are more or less normal in their appearance, you would leave that and tell of something special they did—because it is only in so far as people do something or are something utterly unique that we bother to talk about them at all.

In this following poem, Philip Larkin recounts the total life of a man. Looking through the lens of this poem, it seems we could see every detail of any situation this man could ever get into. Finally we move into the man's head and look out through his eyes, and become aware of his emptiness, his dilemma, his resignation. It is called *Mr Bleaney*, and I think we all recognize him.

> "This was Mr Bleaney's room. He stayed
> The whole time he was at the Bodies, till
> They moved him." Flowered curtains, thin and frayed,
> Fall to within five inches of the sill,
>
> Whose windows show a strip of building land,
> Tussocky, littered. "Mr Bleaney took
> My bit of garden properly in hand."
> Bed, upright chair, sixty-watt bulb, no hook
>
> Behind the door, no room for books or bags—
> "I'll take it." So it happens that I lie
> Where Mr Bleaney lay, and stub my fags
> On the same saucer-souvenir, and try
>
> Stuffing my ears with cotton-wool, to drown
> The jabbering set he egged her on to buy.
> I know his habits—what time he came down,
> His preference for sauce to gravy, why

He kept on plugging at the four aways—
Likewise their yearly frame: the Frinton folk
Who put him up for summer holidays,
And Christmas at his sister's house in Stoke.

But if he stood and watched the frigid wind
Tousling the clouds, lay on the fusty bed
Telling himself that this was home, and grinned,
And shivered, without shaking off the dread

That how we live measures our own nature,
And at his age having no more to show
Than one hired box should make him pretty sure
He warranted no better, I don't know.

Or again, to show the life a person lives, you might select
some simple characteristic situation of their life, and try to
present that. In the following poem of my own, for instance,
I had it in mind to begin with to write a long poem describing
the lives of this husband and wife. But finally, after a good
deal of tinkering about, it boiled down to the single central
situation from which everything else about them, and all the
other events of their relationship seemed to grow. The poem
is about a collier and his wife, and as you will see, it is quite
short. It is called *Her Husband*.

Comes home dull with coal-dust deliberately
To grime the sink and foul towels and let her
Learn with scrubbing brush and scrubbing board
The stubborn character of money.

And let her learn through what kind of dust
He has earned his thirst and the right to quench it
And what sweat he has exchanged for his money
And the blood-count of money. He'll humble her

With new light on her obligations.
The fried, woody chips, kept warm two hours in the oven,
Are only part of her answer.
Hearing the rest, he slams them to the fire-back

49

And is away round the house-end singing
"Come back to Sorrento" in a voice
Of resounding corrugated iron.
Her back has bunched into a hump as an insult . . .

For they will have their rights.
Their jurors are to be assembled
From the little crumbs of soot. Their brief
Goes straight up to heaven and nothing more is heard of it.

So far, we have seen two things then. First, a character is brought alive, close up, as if actually into your presence, by precise descriptive flashes, as in the poem about the girl like a white stone. Second, that a person's whole life can be suggested by recounting one or two typical incidents from it—incidents in which we feel the person's general way of thinking and feeling.

Both these tricks, if they can be called tricks, are the same in principle. The single principle beneath them both is one natural to the workings of the human brain: when we want to convey a complicated scene, or event, or impression, we let one or two details suggest the whole. Nicknames work on the same principle. With a nickname, we generally select some striking details about a person, and ever after call him by that feature. A red-haired boy becomes Ginger—though it is only his hair that is ginger. Or somebody that is always scratching gets to be called Bugs.

You can see how effective and interesting this method is if you make up a short story or poem in which all the people are called not by names, but by something striking in their appearance.

*   *   *   *

Note

In writing imaginatively about people a pupil should be given complete licence. Much has been said about the therapeutic value of uninhibited writing, and though no doubt that can go to the point where mere confusion enters, it is one way of talking about the pleasures and the healing effects of reading and writing poetry.

All imaginative writing is to some extent the voice of what is neglected or forbidden, hence its connection with the past in a nostalgic vein and the future in a revolutionary vein. Hence, too, its connection with the old Adam, with volcanoes, world-endings, monstrous outrages etc. So when an English teacher invites from his pupils imaginative disclosures about people, he generally has School tradition against him. But there ought to be plenty of room within easily permitted things for plenty of interesting work.

Nevertheless, the imagination likes a wide open field of action, fifteen minutes of licence and immunity. If the teacher cannot somehow provide this, he should not expect that much nerve from his pupils.

Dirge

1-2-3 was the number he played but today the number came
    3-2-1;
  bought his Carbide at 30 and it went to 29; had the favourite
    at Bowie but the track was slow—

O, executive type, would you like to drive a floating power, knee-
    action silk-upholstered six? Wed a Hollywood star? Shoot
    the course in 58? Draw to the Ace, King, Jack?
  O, fellow with a will who won't take no, watch out for three
    cigarettes on the same single match; O, democratic voter
    born in August under Mars, beware of liquidated rails—

Denouement to denouement, he took a personal pride in the
    certain, certain way he lived his own private life,
  But nevertheless, they shut off his gas; nevertheless, the bank
    foreclosed; nevertheless, the landlord called; nevertheless,
    the radio broke,

And twelve o'clock arrived just once too often,
   just the same he wore one grey tweed suit, bought one straw
      hat, drank one straight Scotch, walked one short step, took
      one long look, drew one deep breath,
   just one too many,

And wow he died as wow he lived,
   going whop to the office and blooie home to sleep and biff got
      married and bam had children and oof got fired,
   zowie did he live and zowie did he die,

With who the hell are you at the corner of his casket, and where
      the
   hell we going on the right hand silver knob, and who the hell
      cares
   walking second from the end with an American Beauty wreath
      from
   why the hell not,

Very much missed by the circulation staff of the *New York
   Evening Post*; deeply, deeply mourned by the B.M.T.,

Wham, Mr Roosevelt; pow, Sears Roebuck; awk, big dipper;
      bop, summer rain;
   bong, Mr, bong, Mr, bong, Mr, bong.

                                        KENNETH FEARING

Alfred Corning Clark

(1916–1961)

You read the *New York Times*
every day at recess,
but in its dry
obituary, a list
of your wives, nothing is news,

except the ninety-five
thousand dollar engagement ring
you gave the sixth.
Poor rich boy,
you were unseasonably adult
at taking your time,
and died at forty-five.
Poor Al Clark,
behind your enlarged,
hardly recognizable photograph,
I feel the pain.
You were alive. You are dead.
You wore bow-ties and dark
blue coats, and sucked
wintergreen or cinnamon lifesavers
to sweeten your breath.
There must be something—
some one to praise
your triumphant diffidence,
your refusal of exertion,
the intelligence
that pulsed in the sensitive,
pale concavities of your forehead.
You never worked,
and were third in the form.
I owe you something—
I was befogged,
and you were too bored,
quick and cool to laugh.
You are dear to me, Alfred;
our reluctant souls united
in our unconventional
illegal games of chess
on the St Mark's quadrangle.
You usually won—
motionless
as a lizard in the sun.

ROBERT LOWELL

You're

Clownlike, happiest on your hands,
Feet to the stars, and moon-skulled,
Gilled like a fish. A common-sense
Thumbs down on the dodo's mode.
Wrapped up in yourself like a spool,
Trawling your dark as owls do,
Mute as a turnip from the Fourth
Of July to All Fool's day,
O high-riser, my little loaf.

Vague as fog and looked for like mail,
Farther off than Australia.
Bent-backed Atlas, our travelled prawn.
Snug as bud and at home
Like a sprat in a pickle jug.
A creel of eels, all ripples.
Jumpy as a Mexican bean.
Right, like a well-done sum.
A clean slate, with your own face on.

SYLVIA PLATH

Elegy

Her face like a rain-beaten stone on the day she rolled off
With the dark hearse, and enough flowers for an alderman—
And so she was, in her way, Aunt Tilly.

Sighs, sighs, who says they have sequence?
Between the spirit and the flesh—what war?
She never knew;
For she asked no quarter and gave none,
Who sat with the dead when the relatives left,
Who fed and tended the infirm, the mad, the epileptic,
And, with a harsh rasp of a laugh at herself,
Faced up to the worst.

I recall how she harried the children away all the late summer
From the one beautiful thing in her yard, the peach tree;
How she kept the wizened, the fallen, the misshapen for herself,
And picked and pickled the best, to be left on rickety doorsteps.

And yet she died in agony,
Her tongue, at the last, thick, black as an oxen's.

Terror of cops, bill collectors, betrayers of the poor,—
I see you in some celestial supermarket
Moving serenely among the leeks and cabbages,
Probing the squash,
Bearing down, with two steady eyes,
On the quaking butcher.

THEODORE ROETHKE

CHAPTER FOUR

Learning to Think

Now first of all I had better make it quite clear that I am going to talk about a certain kind of thinking. One of the odd wonderful things about this activity we call thinking is that to some extent everybody invents their own brand, has his own way of thinking, not only his own thoughts. You do not ever have to worry that you are not thinking properly— not unless you enter some very specialized job, where a very specialized kind of thinking is required. All you have to do really is think.

And thinking, as we know, is as natural as breathing—some sort of thinking is generally going on in us all the time. So what is all the fuss about? Well, the terrible fact is that though we are all more or less thinking of something or other all the time, some of us are thinking more and some less. Some of us are more energetic about it.

Just as some people are bustling about all the time, getting things done, while others just sit around—so it is inside people's minds—some brains are battling and working and remembering and puzzling things over all the time, or much of the time, and other brains are just lying down snoring and occasionally turning over. Now I am not speaking to that first kind. There is not much I can say to them except wish them good luck. It is to the lazy or secret minds that I am now speaking, and from my own experience I imagine this includes nineteen people out of every twenty. I am one of that clan myself and always have been.

At school, I was plagued by the idea that I really had much better thoughts than I could ever get into words. It was not that I could not find the words, or that the thoughts were too deep or too complicated for words. It was simply that when I tried to speak or write down the thoughts, those thoughts had vanished. All I had was a numb blank feeling, just as if somebody had asked me the name of Julius Caesar's eldest son, or said "7,283 times 6,956—quick. Think, think, think". Now for one reason or another I became very interested in those thoughts of mine that I could never catch. Sometimes they were hardly what you could call a thought—they were a dim sort of feeling about something. They did not fit into any particular subject—history or arithmetic or anything of that sort, except perhaps English. I had the idea, which gradually grew on me, that these were the right sort of thoughts for essays, and yet probably not even essays. But for the most part they were useless to me because I could never get hold of them. Maybe when I was writing an essay I got the tail end of one, but that was not very satisfying.

Now maybe you can see what was happening. I was thinking all right, and even having thoughts that seemed interesting to me, but I could not keep hold of the thoughts, or fish them up when I wanted them. I would think this fact was something peculiar to me, and of interest to nobody else, if I did not know that most people have the same trouble. What thoughts they have are fleeting thoughts—just a flash of it, then gone—or, though they know they know something, or have ideas about something, they just cannot dig those ideas up when they are wanted. Their minds, in fact, seem out of their reach. That is a curious thing to say, but it is quite true.

There is the inner life, which is the world of final reality, the world of memory, emotion, imagination, intelligence, and natural common sense, and which goes on all the time, consciously or unconsciously, like the heart beat. There is also the thinking process by which we break into that inner life and capture answers and evidence to support the answers out of it. That process of raid, or persuasion, or ambush, or dogged hunting, or surrender, is the kind of thinking we have to learn and if we do not somehow learn it, then our minds lie in us like the fish in the pond of a man who cannot fish.

Now you see the kind of thinking I am talking about. Perhaps I ought not to call it thinking at all—it is just that we tend to call everything that goes on in our heads thinking. I am talking about whatever kind of trick or skill it is that enables us to catch those elusive or shadowy thoughts, and collect them together, and hold them still so we can get a really good look at them. I will illustrate what I mean with an example: If you were told, "Think of your uncle"—how long could you hold the idea of your uncle in your head? Right, you imagine him. But then at once he reminds you of something else and you are thinking of that, he has gone into the background, if he has not altogether disappeared. Now get your uncle back. Imagine your uncle and nothing else—nothing whatsoever. After all, there is plenty to be going on with in your uncle, his eyes, what expression? His hair, where is it parted? How many waves has it? What is the exact shade? Or if he is bald, what does the skin feel like? His chin—just how is it? Look at it. As you can see, there is a great deal to your uncle—you could spend hours on him, if you could only keep him in your mind for hours; and when you have looked at him from head to foot, in your memory you have all the memories of what he has said and done, and all your own feelings about him and his sayings and doings. You could spend weeks on him, just holding him there in your mind, and examining the thoughts you have about him. I have exaggerated that, but you see straightway that it is quite difficult to think about your uncle and nothing but your uncle for more than a few seconds. So how can you ever hope to collect all your thoughts about him.

At the same time you obviously could not do that with everything that came into your head—grip hold of it with your imagination, and never let it go till you had studied every grain of it. It would not leave you any time to live. Nevertheless, it is possible to do it for a time. I will illustrate the sort of thing I mean with a poem called *View of a Pig*. In this poem, the poet stares at something which is quite still, and collects the thoughts that concern it.

He does it quite rapidly and briefly, never lifting his eyes from the pig. Obviously, he does not use every thought possible—he chooses the thoughts that fit best together to make a poem. Here is the poem: *View of a Pig*.

The pig lay on a barrow dead.
It weighed, they said, as much as three men.
Its eyes closed, pink white eyelashes.
Its trotters stuck straight out.

Such weight and thick, pink bulk
Set in death seemed not just dead.
It was less than lifeless, further off.
It was like a sack of wheat.

I thumped it without feeling remorse.
One feels guilty insulting the dead,
Walking on graves. But this pig
Did not seem able to accuse.

It was too dead. Just so much
A poundage of lard and pork.
Its last dignity had entirely gone.
It was not a figure of fun.

Too dead now to pity.
To remember its life, din, stronghold
Of earthly pleasure as it had been,
Seemed a false effort, and off the point.

Too deadly factual. Its weight
Oppressed me—how could it be moved?
And the trouble of cutting it up!
The gash in its throat was shocking, but not pathetic.

Once I ran at a fair in the noise
To catch a greased piglet

That was faster and nimbler than a cat,
Its squeal was the rending of metal.

Pigs must have hot blood, they feel like ovens,
Their bite is worse than a horse's—
They chop a half-moon clean out.
They eat cinders, dead cats.

Distinctions and admirations such
As this one was long finished with.
I stared at it a long time. They were going to scald it,
Scald it and scour it like a doorstep.

Now where did the poet learn to settle his mind like that on to one thing? It is a valuable thing to be able to do—but something you are never taught at school, and not many people do it naturally. I am not very good at it, but I did acquire some skill in it. Not in school, but while I was fishing. I fished in still water, with a float. As you know, all a fisherman does is stare at his float for hours on end. I have spent hundreds and hundreds of hours staring at a float—a dot of red or yellow the size of a lentil, ten yards away. Those of you who have never done it, might think it is a very drowsy pastime. It is anything but that.

All the little nagging impulses, that are normally distracting your mind, dissolve. They have to dissolve if you are to go on fishing. If they do not, then you cannot settle down: you get bored and pack up in a bad temper. But once they have dissolved, you enter one of the orders of bliss.

Your whole being rests lightly on your float, but not drowsily: very alert, so that the least twitch of the float arrives like an electric shock. And you are not only watching the float. You are aware, in a horizonless and slightly mesmerized way, like listening to the double bass in orchestral music, of the fish below there in the dark. At every moment your imagination is alarming itself with the size of the thing slowly leaving the weeds and approaching your bait. Or with the world of beauties down there, suspended in total ignorance of you. And the whole purpose of this concentrated excitement, in this arena of apprehension and unforeseeable events, is to bring up some lovely solid thing like living metal from a world where nothing exists but those inevitable facts which raise life out of nothing and return it to nothing.

So you see, fishing with a float is a sort of mental exercise in concentration on a small point, while at the same time letting your imagination work freely to collect everything that might concern that still point: in this case the still point is the float and the things that concern the float are all the fish you are busy imagining. It is not very far from this, you see, to staring steadily at an imagined picture or idea of my uncle and collecting all the thoughts about him that seem to be roaming round my mind, or that come up to look at him. You still find it hard to see how this would work out? Here is a poem about almond trees in Sicily in winter, by D. H. Lawrence. He has extremely interesting thoughts about almond trees and just see how he twines them round his trees—but the trees are always there, he never loses sight of them. *Bare Almond Trees*:

Wet almond-trees, in the rain,
Like iron sticking grimly out of earth;
Black almond trunks, in the rain,
Like iron implements, twisted, hideous out of the earth,
Out of the deep, soft fledge of Sicilian winter-green,
Earth-grass uneatable,
Almond trunks curving blackly, iron-dark, climbing the slopes.

Almond-tree, beneath the terrace rail,
Black, rusted, iron trunk,
You have welded your thin stems finer,
Like steel, like sensitive steel in the air,
Grey, lavender, sensitive steel, curving thinly and brittly up in a
    parabola.

What are you doing in the December rain?
Have you a strange electric sensitiveness in your steel tips?

Do you feel the air for electric influences
Like some strange magnetic apparatus?
Do you take in messages, in some strange code,
From heaven's wolfish, wandering electricity, that prowls so
    constantly round Etna?

Do you take the whisper of sulphur from the air?
Do you hear the chemical accents of the sun?
Do you telephone the roar of the waters over the earth?
And from all this, do you make calculations?
Sicily, December's Sicily in a mass of rain
With iron branching blackly, rusted like old, twisted implements
And brandishing and stooping over earth's wintry fledge, climb-
    ing the slopes
Of uneatable soft green!

Now obviously, not all things we think about keep quite so
still as a dead pig or a tree. Here is another poem of my own
about some sort of goblin creature—I imagine this creature
just discovering that it is alive in the world. It does not know
what it is and is full of questions. It is quite bewildered to
know what is going on. It has a whole string of thoughts, but
at the centre of all of them as you will see, is this creature and
its bewilderment. The poem is called *Wodwo*. A Wodwo is a
sort of half-man half-animal spirit of the forests.

What am I? Nosing here, turning leaves over
following a faint stain on the air to the river's edge
I enter water. What am I to split
the glassy grain of water looking upward I see the bed
of the river above me upside down very clear
what am I doing here in mid-air? Why do I find
this frog so interesting as I inspect its most secret
interior and make it my own? Do these weeds
know me and name me to each other have they
seen me before, do I fit in their world? I seem
separate from the ground and not rooted but dropped
out of nothing casually I've no threads
fastening me to anything I can go anywhere

I seem to have been given the freedom
of this place what am I then? And picking
bits of bark off this rotten stump gives me
no pleasure and it's no use so why do I do it
me and doing that have coincided very queerly
But what shall I be called am I the first
have I an owner what shape am I what
shape am I am I huge if I go
to the end on this way past these trees and past these trees
till I get tired that's touching one wall of me
for the moment if I sit still how everything
stops to watch me I suppose I am the exact centre
but there's all this what is it roots
roots roots roots and here's the water
again very queer but I'll go on looking.

Thinking of one thing like this is not the only way to tackle a problem or to raise your thoughts. Sometimes we want not just our thoughts about this thing, or that thing. We want the progress of thoughts—the way one follows another, as in a story or argument. In other words, we are not then concentrating on one point, but raising one point after another and concentrating on each in turn.

Perhaps you will see that this is the next step, lesson two, after acquiring the skill I have been describing. In a way, the poems that have been read belong to lesson one. It is a very simple lesson, but, as I have said, well worth learning.

*   *   *   *

Note

Without turning English lessons into Yoga sessions it ought to be possible to put the ideas in this chapter into practice fairly easily.

Practice in simple concentration on a small, simple object is the most valuable of all mental exercises. Any object will do. Five minutes at a time is long enough, and one minute is enough to begin with. If the exercise is repeated every lesson, the results will show.

The writing exercise follows from this. The pupil takes any small, simple object, and while concentrating on it gives it the treatment described in the Note to Chapter One: full-out descriptive writing, to a set length, in a set time, in a loose verse form.

The descriptions will be detailed, scientific in their objectivity and microscopic attentiveness.

After some exercises of this sort, the pupil should be encouraged to extend the associations out from the object in every direction, as widely as possible, keeping the chosen object as the centre and anchor of all his statements.

Once the pupil has grasped the possible electrical connections between the objective reality and some words of his, this exercise, which at first might seem dull enough, becomes absorbingly exciting. Even where it produces poor results, the effort towards this kind of perception and description affects the way the pupil looks at, and attends to, everything.

Where this type of exercise can be pursued intensively, the same object should be tackled repeatedly, four or five times, on different days.

Mosquito

When did you start your tricks,
Monsieur?

What do you stand on such high legs for?
Why this length of shredded shank,
You exaltation?

Is it so that you shall lift your centre of gravity upwards
And weigh no more than air as you alight upon me,
Stand upon me weightless, you phantom?

I heard a woman call you the Winged Victory
In sluggish Venice.
You turn your head towards your tail, and smile.

How can you put so much devilry
Into that translucent phantom shred
Of a frail corpus?

Queer, with your thin wings and your streaming legs,
How you sail like a heron, or a dull clot of air,
A nothingness.

Yet what an aura surrounds you;
Your evil little aura, prowling, and casting numbness on my mind.
That is your trick, your bit of filthy magic:
Invisibility, and the anaesthetic power
To deaden my attention in your direction.

But I know your game now, streaky sorcerer.
Queer, how you stalk and prowl the air
In circles and evasions, enveloping me,
Ghoul on wings
Winged Victory.

Settle, and stand on long thin shanks
Eyeing me sideways, and cunningly conscious that I am aware,
You speck.

I hate the way you lurch off sideways into the air
Having read my thoughts against you.

Come then, let us play at unawares,
And see who wins in this sly game of bluff.
Man or mosquito.

You don't know that I exist, and I don't know that you exist.
Now then!

It is your trump,
It is your hateful little trump,
You pointed fiend,
Which shakes my sudden blood in hatred of you:
It is your small, high, hateful bugle in my ear.

Why do you do it?
Surely it is bad policy.
They say you can't help it.

If that is so, then I believe a little in Providence protecting the
    innocent.
But it sounds so amazingly like a slogan,
A yell of triumph as you snatch my scalp.

Blood, red blood
Super-magical
Forbidden liquor.

I behold you stand
For a second enspasmed in oblivion,
Obscenely ecstasied
Sucking live blood,
My blood.

Such silence, such suspended transport,
Such gorging,
Such obscenity of trespass.

You stagger,
As well as you may.
Only your accursed hairy frailty,
Your own imponderable weightlessness
Saves you, wafts you away on the very draught my anger makes
    in its snatching.

Away with a pæan of derision,
You winged blood-drop.

66

Can I not overtake you?
Are you one too many for me?
Winged Victory?
Am I not mosquito enough to out-mosquito you?

Queer what a big stain my sucked blood makes
Beside the infinitesimal faint smear of you!
Queer, what a dim dark smudge you have disappeared into!

D. H. LAWRENCE

My Cat Jeoffry

For I will consider my cat Jeoffry.
For he is the servant of the Living God, duly and daily serving Him.
For at the first glance of the Glory of God in the East he worships in his way.
For is this done by wreathing his body seven times round with elegant quickness.
For then he leaps up to catch the musk, which is the blessing of God on his prayer.
For he rolls upon prank to work it in.
For having done duty, and received blessing, he begins to consider himself.
For this he performs in ten degrees.
For first he looks upon his forepaws to see if they are clean.
For secondly he kicks up behind to clear away there.
For thirdly he works it upon stretch with the forepaws extended.
For fourthly he sharpens his paws by wood.
For fifthly he washes himself.
For sixthly he rolls upon wash.
For seventhly he fleas himself, that he may not be interrupted upon the beat.
For eighthly he rubs himself a-gainst a post.
For ninthly he looks up for his instructions.

For tenthly he goes in quest of food.

For having considered God and himself he will consider his neighbour.

For if he meets another cat he will kiss her in kindness.

For when he takes his prey he plays with it to give it a chance.

For one mouse in seven escapes by his dallying.

For when his day's work is done his business more properly begins.

For he keeps the Lord's watch in the night against the Adversary.

For he counteracts the powers of darkness by his electrical skin and glaring eyes.

For he counteracts the Devil, who is death, by brisking about the life.

For in his morning orisons he loves the sun and the sun loves him.

For he is of the tribe of Tiger.

For the Cherub Cat is a term of the Angel Tiger.

For he has the subtlety and hiss of the serpent, which in goodness he suppresses.

For he will not do destruction, if he is well-fed, neither will he spit without provocation.

For he purrs in thankfulness, when God tells him he's a good Cat.

For he is an instrument for the children to learn benevolence upon.

For every house is incomplete without him and a blessing is lacking in the spirit.

For the Lord commanded Moses concerning the cats at the departure of the Children of Israel from Egypt.

For every family had one cat at least in the bag.

For the English cats are the best in Europe.

For he is the cleanest in the use of his forepaws of any quadrupede.

For the dexterity of his defence is an instance of the love of God to him exceedingly.

For he is the quickest to his mark of any creature.

For he is tenacious of his point.

For he is a mixture of gravity and waggery.

For he knows that God is his Saviour.

For there is nothing sweeter than his peace when at rest.

For there is nothing brisker than his life when in motion.

For he is of the Lord's poor and so indeed is he called by benevolence perpetually—Poor Jeoffry! poor Jeoffry! the rat has bit thy throat.

For I bless the name of the Lord Jesus that Jeoffry is better.

For the divine spirit comes about his body to sustain it in complete cat.

For his tongue is exceeding pure so that it has in purity what it wants in music.

For he is docile and can learn certain things.

For he can set up with gravity which is patience upon approbation.

For he can fetch and carry, which is patience in employment.

For he can jump over a stick which is patience upon proof positive.

For he can spraggle upon waggle at the word of command.

For he can jump from an eminence into his master's bosom.

For he can catch the cork and toss it again.

For he is hated by the hypocrite and miser.

For the former is afraid of detection.

And the latter refuses the charge.

For he camels his back to bear the first notion of business.

For he is good to think on, if a man would express himself neatly.

For he made a great figure in Egypt for his signal services.

For he killed the Ichneumon-rat very pernicious by land.

For his ears are so acute that they sting again.

For from this proceeds the passing quickness of his attention.

For by stroking of him I have found out electricity.

For I perceive God's light about him both wax and fire.

For the electrical fire is the spiritual substance, which God sends from heaven to sustain the bodies of both man and beast.

For God has blessed him in the variety of his movements.

For, tho he cannot fly, he is an excellent clamberer.

For his motions upon the face of the earth are more than any other quadrupede.

For he can tread to all the measures upon the music.

For he can swim for life.

For he can creep.

CHRISTOPHER SMART

Thirteen Ways of Looking at a Blackbird

I

Among twenty snowy mountains
The only moving thing
Was the eye of the blackbird.

II

I was of three minds,
Like a tree
In which there are three blackbirds.

III

The blackbird whirled in the autumn winds.
It was a small part of the pantomime.

IV

A man and a woman
Are one.
A man and a woman and a blackbird
Are one.

V

I do not know which to prefer,
The beauty of inflexions
Or the beauty of innuendos,
The blackbird whistling
Or just after.

VI

Icicles filled the long window
With barbaric glass.
The shadow of the blackbird
Crossed it, to and fro.
The mood
Traced in the shadow
An indecipherable cause.

VII

O thin men of Haddam,
Why do you imagine golden birds.
Do you not see how the blackbird
Walks around the feet
Of the women about you?

VIII

I know noble accents
And lucid, inescapable rhythms;
But I know, too,
That the blackbird is involved
In what I know.

IX

When the blackbird flew out of sight,
It marked the edge
Of one of many circles.

X

At the sight of blackbirds
Flying in a green light
Even the bawds of euphony
Would cry out sharply.

XI

He road over Connecticut
In a glass coach.
Once, a fear pierced him,
In that he mistook
The shadow of his equipage
For blackbirds.

XII

The river is moving.
The blackbird must be flying.

XIII

It was evening all afternoon.
It was snowing
And it was going to snow.
The blackbird sat
In the cedar limbs.

WALLACE STEVENS

Owl

is my favourite. Who flies
like a nothing through the night,
who-whoing. Is a feather
duster in leafy corners ring-a-rosy-ing
boles of mice. Twice

you hear him call. Who
is he looking for? You hear
him hovering over the floor
of the wood. O would you be gold
rings in the driving skull

if you could? Hooded and
vulnerable by the winter suns
owl looks. Is the grain of bark
in the dark. Round beaks are at
work in the pellety nest,

resting. Owl is an eye
in the barn. For a hole
in the trunk owl's blood
is to blame. Black talons in the
petrified fur! Cold walnut hands

on the case of the brain! In the reign
of the chicken owl comes like
a god. Is a goad in

the rain to the pink eyes,
dripping. For a meal in the day

flew, killed, on the moor. Six
mouths are the seed of his
arc in the season. Torn meat
from the sky. Owl lives
by the claws of his brain. On the branch

in the sever of the hand's
twigs owl is a backward look.
Flown wind in the skin. Fine
rain in the bones. Owl breaks
like the day. Am an owl, am an owl.

GEORGE MACBETH

CHAPTER FIVE

Writing about Landscape

What are all those people looking at, sitting on the beach in deck-chairs? They are looking at the sea. But the sea is only the sea, we all know what the sea is like, we do not have to travel two hundred miles, as some of these people have done, just to make sure it is still there. We know it cannot get away.

So what are they all doing there, staring at the sea?

That is what they are doing. They are staring at the sea. They are not talking much, they are not calculating long sums, they are not waiting for a monster to emerge. You ask them what they are doing and they say: "I'm staring at the sea, what do you think I'm doing?"

Of course, some of them might say "We're sunbathing", but how can that be true, why do they have to come all the way to the sea just to sunbathe? They can sunbathe in their backyards if it is only the sun they want. No, they are there on the beach to see the sea first, the sun second, and perhaps the other people third.

If you doubt this, then wait till it begins to rain, and the wind comes up raking the beaches and the promenades with spray. Then the people drive up to the sea as close as they can get in their cars and park there, with their windows shut tight, and their transistors going. They sit eating sandwiches and staring at the sea through the windscreen.

What is it they see in the sea? It is a question not easy to answer.

It is not the ships they are looking for, though they point those out eagerly whenever they appear smoking along the skyline, and it is not tidal waves, which would wash them all away. They do not know what they are looking for. They are sucked to the seaside like pins to a huge magnet, and there they stick. They just like it, it is a pleasure.

People are a bit the same way about any great stretch of scenery. It is better if there is water in it somewhere, but they do not really mind. Most of us have been in a car when the road winds out on to a high exposed point, and we suddenly see a broad sweep of valleys and rivers, or a clear wall of mountains. Everybody gasps. Stop—look! This is so common, you might say inevitable, that local councils make a special pull-in area at the side of the road wherever these points occur, and sometimes you even get ice-cream stands there, all for the lovers of a beautiful view. You leap out of the car or the bus and take aim with your camera.

And we are all familiar with landscape painting. After portraits, I suppose it is the commonest kind of painting. People first, then the view. What a curious fascination landscape must hold for us, if so many of our very greatest painters have spent their lives trying to capture in paint the essence of one landscape after another. And what prices people will pay to hang even very ordinary landscapes, even very dull landscapes, on their living-room walls, like an extra window into some desolate stretch of Connemara, or mudflats with a few wild ducks, or a field with a cow.

Surely it is not that we are all secretly in love with the countryside! But perhaps we are. Who is to say that we are not all secretly in love with grass and trees, preferably out of sight of houses, or if there are houses then they have to be a country style of house, a cottage or a manor. After all, it is a crazy sort of infatuation that makes us hang up in every train compartment four paintings of landscape, when almost certainly all we can see to either side through the huge windows is just more landscape, with all our fellow passengers staring at it. Presumably those four paintings are for when the train gets into the cities and among the buildings that seem to belong to nobody. But even so, why four? Two would be enough.

Whatever it is, we all respond to beauty spots, as we call them. If we do not, it is because we do not like the crowd, and we either find other beauty spots, not yet popular, or we sulk, like children who will not eat at all because they have been refused a sweet, and say we detest the country, and green makes us sick. But on the whole, human beings immediately recognize a beauty spot, and like it.

Usually these places are famous for one thing—they look wild. And the wilder they are, within limits, the more we like them. And what do they do to us? They rest us. People actually come to such places to rest, to recuperate and recover their good spirits. But why cannot they rest in front of their TV or in the town park? Because it is a fact that they cannot.

The thing about these beauty spots, that brings this sense of relaxation and relief, is the state of mind they put us into. These are the remains of what the world was once like all over. They carry us back to the surroundings our ancestors lived in for 150 million years—which is long enough to grow to feel quite at home even in a place as wild as the uncivilized earth. Civilization is comparatively new, it is still a bit of a strain on our nerves—it is not quite a home to mankind yet, we still need occasional holidays back in the old surroundings. It is only there that the ancient instincts and feelings in which most of our body lives can feel at home and on their own ground. It is almost as though these places were generators where we can recharge our run-down batteries. And what do we recharge with, what sort of electricity? Those prehistoric feelings, satisfactions we are hardly aware of except as a sensation of pleasure—these are like a blood transfusion to us, and in wild surroundings they rise to the surface and refresh us, renew us. For some people, even to think about such places is a refreshment.

And perhaps this is why we are so often pleased to find such places represented in paintings or in writing—they revive in us these feelings which are as essential to our health as water is to plants.

Here is a passage by the poet Edward Thomas, which shows pretty clearly what I mean. It is not a poem, or at least it is not in verse. It is a description of the sea, and he evidently is aware of just those feelings I have been talking about, as he encounters it in the early morning. I believe this is a good account of the reaction most people have to the sea in one of its most characteristic moods.

The sea . . . has not changed and shrunken and grown like the earth; it is not sunwarmed: it is a monster that has lain unmoved by time, sleeping and moaning outside the gates within which men and animals have become what they are. Actually that cold fatal element and its myriad population without a sound brings a wistfulness into the mind as if it could feel back dimly and recall the dawn of time when the sea was incomprehensible and impassable, when the earth had but lately risen out of the waters and was yet again to descend beneath: it becomes a type of the waste where everything is unknown or uncertain except death, pouring into the brain the thoughts that men have had on looking out over untrodden mountain, forest, swamp, in the drizzling dawn of the world. The sea is exactly what it was when mountain, forest, swamp were imperturbable enemies, and the sight of it restores the ancient fear. I remember one dawn above all others when this restoration was complete. When it was yet dark the wind rose gustily under a low grey sky and a lark sang amidst the moan of gorse and the creak of gates and the deeply taken breath of the tide at the full. Nor was it yet light when the gulls began to wheel and wind and float with a motion like foam on a whirl-pool or interwoven snow. They wheeled about the masts of fishing boats that nodded and kissed and crossed in a steep cove of crags whose black edges were slavered by the foam of the dark sea; and there were no men among the boats or about the grey houses that looked past the walls of the cove to the grim staircase and sea-doors of a black headland, whose perpendicular rocks stood up . . . in the likeness of gigantic idols. The high crags were bushy and scaly with lichen, and they were cushioned upon thrift and bird's foot trefoil and white bladder campion. It was a bristling sea, not in the least stormy, but bristling, dark and cold through the slow, colourless dawn, dark and cold and im-

77

mense; and at the edge of it the earth knelt, offering up the music of a small flitting bird and the beauty of small flowers, white and gold, to those idols. They were terrible enough. But the sea was more terrible. . . .

What really makes this passage so powerful in its effect, for me at least, is that eerie account of the sea's overshadowing of the lark and the gates and the boats and the gulls and the small flowers—those small vital things, the very opposites to the immense, dead, dark sea.

And this is what makes landscapes valuable to us: not simply the presence of the elements, but the encounter between the elemental things and the living, preferably the human. It is, as I said before, the presence of human feeling, what human feeling the landscape makes us conscious of. Take this sentence: 1,500 acres, mixed parkland and beech forest, with spacious lake and distant view of Chilterns. What does this mean to us? Almost nothing. It sounds like a poor advertisement. But when those same acres appear in a painting by the English artist, Turner—it may well be one of the places you will never forget, he has shown it to us through a lens of powerful, rich feeling.

It is quite difficult to describe a landscape in words, of course. Even in a small field, there is infinitely too much to render in anything like the completeness that even the swiftest watercolour can. But words can render the feeling. In this next piece, for instance, see how vivid a picture you can imagine: the poem is called *Virginia*, one of the States in the North American deep south, and it is by T. S. Eliot.

> Red river, red river,
> Slow flow heat is silence
> No will is still as a river
> Still. Will heat move
> Only through the mocking-bird
> Heard once? Still hills
> Wait. Gates wait. Purple trees,
> White trees, wait, wait,

> Delay, decay. Living, living,
> Never moving. Ever moving
> Iron thoughts came with me
> And go with me:
> Red river, river, river.

If you are anything like me, you will have an intensely vivid impression of a place from that poem. You feel you could paint it. And yet what does it describe? Are the purple trees near the white trees? Are those gates garden gates or field gates? Are the gates near the trees or near the river? Are there houses or not? Are the trees beside the river? Or on the hills? The poem does not say. Then how does it create so strong a picture? It creates so vivid a picture, as did the other passage, by creating an intensely vivid feeling. What the poem does describe is a feeling of slowness, with a prevailing stillness, of suspended time, of heat, and dryness, and fatigue, with an undertone of oppressive danger, like a hot afternoon that will turn to thunder and lightning, a lazy day in the derelict deep south. Everything is in the slow winding progress of the phrases. Perhaps a good way to grasp it is to think of it as the words of the river describing its own sunken progress through this heat-stupefied land. The hills, the gates, the white trees, the purple trees, they all go over, moving yet still, like reflections on the surface, under which the river is slowly journeying.

> . . . Living, living,
> Never moving. Ever moving
> Iron thoughts came with me
> And go with me: . . .

In this next poem there is much more of what we might call straightforward description, but the vivid details are all aiming one way: it is a scene in sharp focus: all gloom and brilliance, the exhilaration and uneasy sunniness of a bleak, rather lonely place. It is the closest thing to a conventional beauty spot that I know of in poetry. And it is so clean and right that whenever

I see anything like it in actual scenery I think—"It's almost as good as *Inversnaid*" which is the title of this poem by Gerard Manley Hopkins.

> This darksome burn, horseback brown,
> His rollrock highroad roaring down,
> In coop and in comb the fleece of his fóam
> Flutes and low to the lake falls home.
>
> A windpuff-bonnet of fawn-froth
> Turns and twindles over the broth
> Of a pool so pitchblack, fell-frowning,
> It rounds and rounds Despair to drowning.
>
> Degged with dew, dappled with dew
> Are the groins of the braes that the brook treads through,
> Wiry heathpacks, flitches of fern,
> And the beadbonny ash that sits over the burn.
>
> What would the world be, once bereft
> Of wet and of wildness? Let them be left,
> O let them be left, wildness and wet;
> Long live the weeds and the wilderness yet.

The value of such poems is that they are better, in some ways, than actual landscapes. The feelings that come over us confusedly and fleetingly when we are actually in the places, are concentrated and purified and intensified in these poems. There is a feeling very common among people who occasionally get the impulse to write poetry, when they see some striking scene, or feel the unique atmosphere of some place, they have a strong desire to capture it in some way, to single out and lay hold of the essential thing in it, to feel out and grasp the full delight of it. With landscapes this is a difficult thing to do, because they contain so many details, they present us with so much evidence, we may well be overwhelmed, because all we want are those few key things that open up our human excitement, our deepest feeling of the place. We do not want a photograph, we want a film with exactly the right music, and the music is the most important.

In this next poem there is even more visual description than in that last piece. But each image does two things: it projects some detail of the scene, like a camera shot, at the same time as it defines the way you are to feel about that shot. Just as the music in a film works on our feelings far more strongly than pictures—though without the pictures we should probably find most of the music of very little interest, and without the music the pictures would have a hard job holding our attention, let alone moving us. This is a description of walking on the moors above Wuthering Heights, in West Yorkshire, towards nightfall. Not a description of the moors, as I say, but of what it feels like to be walking over them. The poem is by the American poet, Sylvia Plath. *Wuthering Heights.*

> The horizons ring me like faggots,
> Tilted and disparate, and always unstable.
> Touched by a match, they might warm me,
> And their fine lines singe
> The air to orange
> Before the distances they pin evaporate,
> Weighting the pale sky with a solider colour.
> But they only dissolve and dissolve
> Like a series of promises, as I step forward.
>
> There is no life higher than the grasstops
> Or the hearts of sheep, and the wind
> Pours by like destiny, bending
> Everything in one direction.
> I can feel it trying
> To funnel my heat away.
> If I pay the roots of the heather
> Too close attention, they will invite me
> To whiten my bones among them.
>
> The sheep know where they are,
> Browsing in their dirty wool-clouds,

Grey as the weather,
The black slots of their pupils take me in.
It is like being mailed into space,
A thin silly message.
They stand about in grandmotherly disguise,
All wig curls and yellow teeth
And hard, marbly baas.

I come to wheel ruts and water
Limpid as the solitudes
That flee through my fingers.
Hollow doorsteps go from grass to grass;
Lintel and sill have unhinged themselves.
Of people the air only
Remembers a few odd syllables.
It rehearses them moaningly:
Black stone, black stone.

The sky leans on me, me, the one upright
Among all horizontals.
The grass is beating its head distractedly.
It is too delicate
For a life in such company;
Darkness terrifies it.
Now, in valleys narrow
And black as purses, the house lights
Gleam like small change.

*   *   *   *

Note

The poems quoted in this chapter will give clues, but it is a mistake, I think, to expect children to write excitedly about landscape in a style as impersonal as in these. In my experience, the most productive method is to release the pupil, as it were, in some special setting, and let them write the monologue of their journey. It will usually be found that children write more rewardingly—both for themselves and for the reader—about strange or extreme landscapes than about anything they know well. It is as if what they know well can only become imagination, and available to the pen, when they have somehow left it. Deserts, steppes, the Antarctic, the moon, all come more easily than the view from their bedroom window.

Here are seven subjects from which at different times I got results.

The main thing to keep in mind is that the details should be kept sharp and special.

1. I am a giant octopus. A tidal wave has carried me into the wrong sea—too cold. I am trying to find my way home over the sea-floor.
2. I am a hermit or castaway on an island in the far Southern Atlantic. I do nothing but search for food.
3. I am a creature from outer space. I have landed near the sea. This is my report to H.Q.
4. I am the Amazon.
5. What can you see through this telescope?
6. I am blind. Once, for just five minutes, I could see. This is what I saw.
7. I am an escaped prisoner being hunted by dogs.

Sailing to an Island

The boom above my knees lifts, and the boat
Drops, and the surge departs, departs, my cheek
Kissed and rejected, kissed, as the gaff sways
A tangent, cuts the infinite sky to red
Maps, and the mast draws eight and eight across
Measureless blue, the boatmen sing or sleep.

We point all day for our chosen island,
Clare, with its crags purpled by legend;
There under castles the hot O'Malleys,
Daughters of Granuaile, the pirate queen

Who boarded a Turk with a blunderbuss,
Comb red hair and assemble cattle.
Across the shelved Atlantic groundswell
Plumbed by the sun's kingfisher rod,
We sail to locate in sea, earth and stone
The myth of a shrewd and brutal swordswoman
Who piously endowed an abbey.
Seven hours we try against wind and tide,
Tack and return, making no headway.
The north wind sticks like a gag in our teeth.

Encased in a mirage, steam on the water,
Loosely we coast where hideous rocks jag,
An acropolis of cormorants, an extinct
Volcano where spiders spin, a purgatory
Guarded by hags and bristled with breakers.

The breeze as we plunge slowly stiffens:
There are hills of sea between us and land,
Between our hopes and the island harbour.
A child vomits. The boat veers and bucks.
There is no refuge on the gannet's cliff.
We are far, far out: the hull is rotten,
The spars are splitting, the rigging is frayed,
And our helmsman laughs uncautiously.
What of those who must earn their living
On the ribald face of a mad mistress?
We in holiday fashion know
This is the boat that belched its crew
Dead on the beach in the Cleggan disaster.

Now she dips and the sail hits the water.
She hoves to a squall; is struck; and shudders.
Someone is shouting. The boom, weak as scissors,
Has snapped, the boatman is praying.
Orders thunder and canvas cannonades.
She smothers in spray. We still have a mast;
The oar makes a boom. I am told to cut
Cords out of fishing lines, fasten the jib.

Ropes lash my cheeks. Ease! Ease at last:
She swings to leeward, we can safely run.

Washed over rails our Clare island dreams,
With storm behind us we straddle the wakeful
Waters that draw us headfast to Inishbofin.

The bows rock as she overtakes the surge.
We neither sleep nor sing nor talk,
But look to the land where the men are mowing.
What will the islanders think of our folly?
The whispering spontaneous reception committee
Nods and smokes by the calm jetty.
Am I jealous of these courteous fishermen
Who hand us ashore, for knowing the sea
Intimately, for respecting the storm
That took nine of their men on one bad night
And five from Rossadillisk in this very boat?
Their harbour is sheltered. They are slow to tell
The story again. There is local pride
In their home-built ships.
We are advised to return next day by the mail.

But tonight we stay, drinking with people
Happy in the monotony of boats,
Bringing the catch to the Cleggan market,
Cultivating fields, or retiring from America
With enough to soak till morning or old age.

The bench below my knees lifts, and the floor
Drops, and the words depart, depart, with faces
Blurred by the smoke. An old man grips my arm,
His shot eyes twitch, quietly dissatisfied.
He has lost his watch, an American gold
From Boston gas-works. He treats the company
To the secretive surge, the sea of his sadness.
I slip outside, fall among stones and nettles,
Crackling dry twigs on an elder tree,
While an accordion drones above the hill.

Later, I reach a room, where the moon stares
Cobwebbed through the window. The tide has ebbed,
Boats are careened in the harbour. Here is a bed.

RICHARD MURPHY

CHAPTER SIX

Writing a Novel: Beginning

We all tell stories. We all recount odd incidents that have happened to us. In so far as we talk at all we are generally telling something of a story. Some of us go further and make stories up at great length, imagine how it would be if this or that happened to us, what would follow, what would happen next and next. In fact you could not live if you were not continually making up little stories. When you cross a road you hesitate and make sure everything is clear. You do this because a little story has run along in your head and shown you a car coming, screeching its brakes, swerving to miss you, bouncing off the far wall, probably turning over three times and bursting its doors and spilling out people and collie dogs, etc. . . . quite a hectic little tale, and it goes through your head in a flash, so quickly and lightly that you are hardly aware of it. Or when there is anything you want very much you are making up a story all the time of how you will get it and how it will be, and sometimes you put yourself through that kind of story almost as if you were living it. Sometimes you get quite lost in it and come back to yourself with a start.

Well, that is natural enough, and I only mention it to put you in mind of your natural gifts, so that what I am going to propose will not seem so difficult. And what I am going to propose is that you write a novel.

As you know, the practical advantages of being able to write out your thoughts fluently are very great. For one thing, when you are used to writing them out, they present themselves, one after another. When you are not used to writing them out, they mill around among themselves usually and you see nothing but heads and tails of them when you sit down to get them on paper. I know from my own experience that the first two or three hours of every exam I ever took were spent simply getting my pen warmed up, and by then it was too late. All this is quite apart from the intense pleasure to be had from writing itself, once you have let yourself go.

At the same time you will find reading becomes more interesting, as you begin to understand some of the difficulties and arts of writing, which you inevitably will.

And though it seems strange to say so, even life becomes more interesting, because one thing that writing teaches to most of us is that we are not looking at things as closely as we ought to and we are not understanding them as deeply as we ought. It is perhaps only when you sit down to write out, say, an account of the most interesting thing that has happened to you since Christmas that you realize you remember almost nothing of it: you cannot remember seeing what people wore, what they did exactly, what they said exactly. Most of us just retain a vague impression of an event, with one or two details that affected us directly, and when we ask someone else to give their account of the same event it is highly probable that their memory will contradict ours. This could mean we both saw different aspects of the event and are both, in our way, right. But it is certain that we both saw almost nothing and made our judgment of all the facts after only seeing one or two of them. How would you like to be condemned by a jury who when they go into the jury room remember about as much of your case as you do of the lessons you had last week?

In this noisy, busy, easy modern life, we are bombarded by sights and sounds that have no important meaning for us . . . either they are utterly meaningless, like traffic noises, or they simply entertain us, like TV noises. And so we develop lazy habits of not really listening and not really looking, just letting it all slide off us, knowing that it does not really matter whether we see or hear these things or not . . . we shall not get hurt and we shall not go hungry.

And so most of us drift through life not really attending to anything, like fat grampuses in an aquarium, where there are no sharks and no killer whales, where the keeper brings all the food we need, where the people on the other side of the glass are creatures from another world and do not matter at all. That is the way most of us are by the time we are eighteen or nineteen or so, and the only thing that troubles us then is boredom.

I recently read an account of an experiment. A film of a submarine manœuvring under water was shown to a mixed audience of Americans and African tribesmen. America, as you know, is a fat easy country, like England. Africa is not: for most Africans life is still terribly hard, and if they do not keep as wide awake to their surroundings as animals, they are finished. After the film was shown, the people in the audience were asked to write out what they had seen. What do you think the results were like?

The Americans, as I have said, live much as we do, they look at things much as we do. From their accounts you would think they had seen almost nothing . . . they had seen a submarine, of course, moving. But what moves it made for the most part they were not sure, and you could not guess what kind of a submarine they had seen or whether it was even under water. The African accounts were quite different. The Africans, almost to a man, had seen every single thing and remembered it . . . the shape of the submarine, all its visible fittings; they described its movements precisely; they described in detail the appearance of the water and the sea-floor over which the submarine moved. You would think their lives depended on it. What do you think your account would be like?

Now in this novel which you are going to write you will be able to practise these things: first of all, simply writing, or rather letting your imagination go and following it with your pen as fast as you can, and keeping this up till it may become second nature to you. Secondly you will be able to practise your observation, and no doubt most of you will find yourselves going to look at certain things again and more closely than you did before when you find them cropping up in your novel. If a thing or a person or a place does not seem real in your writing, then it or he or she just is not there. And the whole point of writing about things and people and places is to present them as they actually are, to make a record of them for your readers. So every page in your novel will be a new exercise in observation, till pretty soon, we hope, something approaching photographic observation begins to come naturally to you.

Probably you are worried about the story, how are you going to keep it up, novels go on so long. It is really much easier than you think. Once you have got it going it will invent itself, it will begin to think for you, and some of you, I have no doubt, will find you can hardly stop it. Characters will push their way into it, and lead you into all kinds of situations and unexpected corners. The only thing for you is to let it grow, like a freakish giant marrow that will not stop, and to follow it with your pen; and you need not try to look too far ahead.

The one bit of technical advice, to set you off, is this: the novel must be written in chapters and these can be as short as you like. Only a couple of pages, if you like. Chapters make it easier for you to concentrate on one stage of the action at a time, or one incident at a time. And it means that you can make up the whole novel out of the most interesting parts of your story. Any necessary but boring bits, you simply miss out between chapters and mention in a sentence or two at the start of the next chapter. So a chapter might start: "Willie Weasel-cheeks lay there in bed for the next three weeks recovering from his fright, and every morning his mother brought in hot coffee and a poached egg and every lunchtime when she brought his lunch she carried away the cold coffee and the stale poached egg which he hadn't touched, and he hadn't touched them because it was one result of his fright that Willie couldn't stand coffee and the sight of a poached egg brought him out in a cold sweat. But his mother wouldn't be told and so morning after morning she brought him in these things.

And this went on until the Monday morning of the fourth week when instead of coffee and eggs she brought a telegram . . . etc." Then things start up again, you see, with the news in the telegram.

So to begin with there are only two things for you to keep in mind. Do not be frightened of following wherever the story leads, and keep your eyes and your ears open: see everything, hear everything, and get it down in the words.

The best beginning of all for a story you are going to write is one you have written yourself, but for those of you who find it hard to get started here are a few sample beginnings.

The Creature

Since three that afternoon it had eaten six eggs, a pound of sausages, a slipper and a small sheepskin carpet. But now she was going to fix it. She would give it something to settle it and put it to sleep, stop its scrabblings and whinings with a really solid meal.

So, keeping the Christmas pudding under a towel in case anybody should come out and ask her what she was doing wandering about the house at that hour, Annabelle climbed the stair. She stepped close to the wall, because she knew that every single step creaked out like a mouse if you stepped on the end near the banister. It was long past midnight. Like a ghost, almost frightening herself, she crept past her parents' bedroom and let herself into her own. The door closed behind her with a sharp click.

Now, snapping on the light, she kneeled beside the bed, drew an old dog-eared brown suitcase from under it and opened the lid.

"Shhh!" she hissed as the green bony crocodile head, with its eyes like sucked yellow fruit-gums, reared up at her on its snaky neck, whining like a puppy dog. And to silence the creature she threw aside the towel and set the pudding down in the suitcase.

"Shhh!" she hissed again, to the gulpings and bubblings

and slurpings and suckings and puffings that followed. But he took no notice, and she sat almost in tears as he devoured the dense blackish uncooked Christmas pudding, label and all. What was she going to do with him? How was she going to feed him?

"And you've grown nearly six inches," she whispered bitterly, "since three o'clock this afternoon."

The Escape

He landed at the bottom of the wall with a thud and crouched. So far so good. He listened, feeling his ears move on his head as he strained to pick up the sounds of the guards on the wall top. Complete silence. Had they heard him then? Even now, they were probably peering down at him, taking aim. He waited, narrowing his eyes as if that might make him less visible.

He had chosen a moonless night, but the starlight was brighter than he had wanted it. The wide field between himself and the blackness of the woods half a mile away seemed bright as a floodlit football pitch. Looking up, he could see the blackly projecting buttress under the machine-gun post. Farther along, though he could not see it, he knew the searchlight was glaring down into the courtyard behind the wall, poking into every corner and fingering over the cindered paths. He had evaded that so far, but now, if he made one careless move, it could easily swing round and pick him up again outside the prison, exposing him to the machine-gunners.

He flattened to the wall and held his breath. Footsteps were coming along the wall top, slowly, casually. He thought of the spiders, safely hidden in the cracks of the wall.

Directly above him the footsteps stopped. He heard the low voices of the guards.

The New Home

The curtains were not up yet and she stood at the front window looking out through the bare panes. It was like no place she had ever seen. And she did not know whether she liked it. Her old life, her old friends, were far away on the other side of England. Here she knew no one, she was a stranger, a newcomer. And she did not know whether she liked this house either, with its locked attic, its fusty cellars full of rusty mouldy junk other people had left there, its bare floors and echoing staircase . . . for no carpets had been put down yet.

Her mother came into the room and startled her out of her dream.

"We need some drawing-pins. Here's a shilling, go and find a shop. Hurry up, we want to get the bedrooms ready."

And so she found herself in the street. What was this life going to be like? Where were her new friends?

First of all, where was the shop?

Some Sort of Men

My brother kept on shouting but I took no notice. He had been doing that all morning, going off among the rocks on his own, then shouting for me to come, and when I got up to him he would look at me as if I were silly and say, "What do you want?", so now I took no notice of him and went on searching for shells. As each wave ran back out over the pebbles I followed it, because there, right under the breakers, is the very best place for new shells.

I do not know what made me look up. Perhaps it was that my brother had stopped shouting. The silence made me look up. But when I looked over to where he had been I started shouting myself. Three short black figures had appeared from somewhere and were dragging him towards the cliff. They were so short and queerly lumpish that I thought at first they must be big chimpanzees, but as I ran towards them I saw their belts and boots and beards. They were men all right, some sort of men.

"Stop, stop, let him go," I shouted.

When they heard my voice they lifted him clear of the

ground and began to run, leaping from rock to rock while I had to scramble down them and up and over, tripping and hacking my shins, and I was still fifty yards behind when all four disappeared into a crevice at the bottom of the cliff. I got there panting and shouted in after them, "Dennis, Dennis," hoping that he would hear and shout back. I had expected the crevice to be the entrance of a sort of cave, you see. I was wrong. The crevice went in no more than four feet and ended in solid rock. And it was quite empty.

The Other Side of the Hill

"We're off now."

"They'll never catch us."

"We'll never go back till we're rich."

The three of them sat on the hilltop and looked down at the town, a dark reeking pit, where the first lights were glowing like embers in a raked-out campfire. They had already come over a mile. And on the other side of the hill lay . . .

Well, Brian knew. With his thin legs like a linnet and his great brain behind spectacles like oyster shells, he had it all worked out. He knew just what roots and leaves you could eat and which would stretch you out like a cod on a slab. He knew the constellations and so could tell which direction to travel in at night. He said he knew how to make a fire by rubbing sticks together and what sort of wood these sticks had to be. He had read how to make a canoe out of a log, by burning it hollow with little fires. The other two, Bert and Bloodnut, trusted him completely.

"When shall we eat?" asked Bert. "We've got to keep our strength up."

He had cheese and a tin of tongue. Bloodnut had a packet of dates and a banana. Brian had nothing.

"Eat?" demanded Brian indignantly. "Eat? Tonight we've got to keep going. They'll be out after us by eleven. We want to be far away by morning. Safe. Then we can eat. Then we'll hunt something."

Bloodnut fingered the shilling in his pocket. He was already wishing he had bought a meat pie.

"Come on." Brian got up. The other two got up. Brian looked up at the sky but there were no stars yet. He led off in the direction away from the town.

The Story of a Story

There was once a story

It ended
Before its beginning
And began
After its end

Its heroes entered it
After their death
And left it
Before their birth

Its heroes spoke
Of some world of some sky
They said all kinds of things

Only they did not say
What they did not know themselves
That they were only heroes from a story

From a story that ends
Before its beginning

And begins
After it has ended

VASCO POPA
(translated by Anne Pennington)

CHAPTER SEVEN

Writing a Novel: Going On

There is no correct way to write a novel, or rather, there is only one, and that one way is to make it interesting. That is very easily said, but how do you make your writing interesting? Surely this is what all the thousands of writers all over the world are trying to find out, how they can make their writing interesting.

The answer to the question is, that you write interestingly only about the things that genuinely interest you. This is an infallible rule.

One writer will be interested in people and all the details of their doings, and so his novel is full of conversations, he describes his characters carefully and their emotions, their hopes and fears, and the reader catches his excitement in these things. Whatever the writer feels in putting down the words is what the reader feels in reading them. Now if that same writer tried to write about something that he personally finds dull and boring, then his writing becomes dull and boring. For instance, an attack of giant rats could be made very interesting indeed. But to make it interesting you would need a writer who gets excited about giant rats, and not all writers are that sort. On the other hand, plenty of writers are interested in both people and giant rats and so could write interestingly about both, and probably a great many other things too. But every writer's genuine interests are limited at some point and if he tries to write about things beyond that point, his writing becomes cold as if the hot tap had been turned off and only the cold left running.

Now when you are writing a novel, or a long rambling story,

you are constantly thinking of what is coming up next, and there occasionally arrives a time when it seems to you that nothing comes next—you dry up, you run out of ideas. This is the commonest difficulty among writers who write long stories. Even if they are the sort that plan out every incident ahead, they are sometimes brought to a stop, and their next incident somehow will not go, it will not come to life, it no longer seems the right thing, and they are stuck. This is a sign that the story has led them outside their genuine interests, it has lured them on over the boundary into country that they have no real feeling for. It is as if their brains said: "We have nothing to say about this, we don't know anything about it and we don't feel anything about it and it bores us." Now, I am going to suppose that you have all reached this point. You are beating your brains. What comes next? Where is your idea to come from? That is the important question. Where is your next idea to come from?

You sit feeling bored. Then a sly notion comes into your head, you remember something in a book you read—and away you go using that hint from somebody else's book. That is very common. But it is fatal. It is common because what has already been written about by somebody else is very easy to write about again, the hard work has been done for you. It is like food you do not need to chew. But as I say, it is fatal. It is fatal because you are no longer using your own excitement, your own experience and interest, you are merely serving up somebody else's cold. Your writing becomes dull, and you yourself deep down wonder why you are bothering to carry on with it.

So beware. As you sit there chewing your pen, brought to a full stop, wondering what comes next, do not be cheated into rushing after something you have read. All right, what are you to go after?

Now I have said that you must write only about what genuinely interests you. But, you reply, you are interested in so many things and that does not seem to make them easy to write about. That is because most of these interests, as you call them, are only casual interests, not genuine interests. But how are we to know the difference between the two? What is the difference?

When we are born we have one great genuine interest: food. We have a smaller interest, also genuine, in warmth. These are genuine interests because our whole life is bound up in them. If we are not fed, we howl and eventually die. If we get too cold, we howl and eventually, if nothing is done about it, we die. These are what you might call passionate interests. And at that age, we have no casual interests.

But by the time we are six months old, our interests have developed. We still have the great main genuine interest in being fed, and our genuine interest in warmth. But now we have several casual interests: in light, for instance. And in the faces of our mother and father. We stare at these, we smile when they appear. But that is all. We are curious about them, a little. But as soon as they disappear we forget about them and return to our true interests in food and warmth.

Now compare these to our interests at ten years old. Food, of course, and warmth, are strong as ever, but by now our interest in the faces of our mother and father is no longer casual, it is genuine, bound up with our whole life, as is everything else about those two important people. Our emotions are too deeply involved with them ever to be untangled. And that first casual interest in light has become our infinitely more complicated set of interests in everything we see around us, all in turn tangled up with other interests that have sprung up in the meantime, our interest in certain people, certain places, certain pleasures, certain duties. By now we have many genuine interests, many things that have become so deeply a part of us that we cannot easily imagine what our life would be without them and we cannot bear to think of losing them. At the same time, we have scores of casual interests, things we are curious to investigate further, and there are more every week, and when we look a bit more closely we see that these casual interests are like the buds where a genuine interest may

98

eventually grow. As we follow up a casual interest, and investigate the thing, and find it more and more fascinating, and learn more about it, our emotions become involved with it as it sinks into us. We feel we get to know it, it begins to link up with our other knowledge and soon that thing too is woven into our lives so deeply that we may even feel slightly resentful when we hear it mentioned by other people. And so what was first a casual interest has become a genuine interest. And this is happening all the time, in every direction, and this is how we grow. In this way we get to know people, places, skills, and facts. And these genuine interests, these things about which you have real private feelings and real experience, are the only things you will be able to write about.

So, in writing, you have to be able to distinguish between those things about which you are merely curious—things you heard about last week or read about yesterday—and things which are a deep part of your life. Some people are better at making this distinction than others. The difference between a fairly interesting writer and a fascinating writer is that the fascinating writer has a better nose for what genuinely excites him, he is hotter on the trail, he has a better instinct for what is truly alive in him. The worse writer may seem to be more sensible in many ways, but he is less sensible in this vital matter: he cannot quite distinguish what is full of life from what is only half full or empty of it. And so his writing is less alive, and as a writer he is less alive, and in writing, as in everything else, nothing matters but life.

But you have the advantage of being still quite young. The younger you are, the easier it is to know what you genuinely like and what you genuinely do not like, what is important to you and what is not. As you grow older a thousand considerations complicate matters, it becomes more and more difficult to sort out the living from the half living and the dead, but for you it is still fairly easy. So, as you sit there, completely dried up, at a dead end, beating your brains, bored, looking for an idea, cursing this novel you have got yourself into, you ask yourself: "What can I use next?" You are not working out an arithmetical problem. In this story you are free to amuse yourself. So you say: "What can I set on fire next? What genuine interest of mine can I plunge into now and really let myself go? What part of my life would I die to be separated from?" There is an answer, and at once, disguising it as much or as little as you please, you turn your story that way. Or what would you most like to see happen? Or where do you long to be? Or what do you fear—because your fears are as deep as your loves, and just as inspiring.

If you were writing a book to be published, things might not be so easy. You might be restrained by the fear that your wild imaginings might drive some people crazy, or that the people you are writing about might recognize themselves in your story and sue you for thousands of pounds. As it is, you are free, you can go off in any direction whatsoever, so long as the flame in your mind burns that way.

Your genuine interests are the clue to your genuine feelings, like floats over sunken lobster-pots, and it is those feelings you are after, because it is those living feelings that we other people, your readers, are interested in. Whatever else you may be told, the fact remains that writing is made out of feelings. As you are using words, you also have to use thoughts and pictures because words are made of thoughts and pictures. If you were writing music, you would have to use notes and instruments. If you were painting a picture, you would have to use paints and canvas or paper. But these are dead things until feeling flows through them, and the feeling comes out of you, in this case, and do not think there is any end of it. And the more you search for it, the more of it you find.

When Balzac, the great French novelist, was writing, he used to rave about his room, shouting and muttering and pouring with sweat. On one occasion, imagining the anguish of one of his characters, he tore a bedspread to pieces with his teeth. He gave everything he had, you see, though that is not the only way to do it.

CHAPTER EIGHT

Meet My Folks

Are your relatives a nuisance? Perhaps you are like a person I know, whose life is absolutely swamped by brothers, sisters, uncles, aunts and cousins. The trouble with relatives is, you did not choose them and now you cannot change them: you are stuck with them, whether you like them or not. And they seem to think they own you as if you were their pet cat or something of that sort. They feel they have a right to know all about what you are doing, and if they do not like it they say, "You'll have to stop that", and they begin to give you advice. They can be a nuisance.

On the other hand, they can be endlessly interesting, and to a writer nothing is quite so interesting or important as his relatives. Now why should this be so?

All writers agree, you cannot write about something for which you have no feeling. Unless something interests or excites you or belongs to your life in a deep way, then you just cannot think of anything to say about it. The words will not come. Now, unless you are an unusual person, you will never in this world get to know anybody quite as well as you know your relatives, and your feelings will never be tied up with anybody or with anything quite so deeply as it is with them. Accordingly, most writers find they have plenty to say about their relatives. And these feelings we have for our relatives are not unshakeably fixed to those particular people. This is one of the curious facts about feelings. If we get on well with our brother, we tend to be attracted to make friends with boys or men who remind us of our brother, and begin to feel that this new friendship is somehow using the feeling we originally had for our brother alone. In the same way, if you are a writer, and you invent a character who reminds you in some way of your brother, then all your old feelings about your brother flow into this invented character and help to bring it to life. Some very great writers have written their best books in this way, re-arranging their relatives in imagination, under different names and appearances of course.

It is not always completely easy. Our feelings about some of our relatives, particularly about our mother and father, are so complicated and so deeply rooted that they may be just too much for a writer to manage, and he finds he cannot say a thing about them. In writing these poems of mine about relatives, I found it almost impossible to write about the mother. Now these people in my poems are not my real relatives, they are members of a family I was inventing. Nevertheless, when it came to inventing a mother, I found it impossible to write about such a person in the style in which these poems are written. I was stuck. My feelings about my mother, you see, must be too complicated to flow easily into words. I ended up writing a poem that left me quite unsatisfied. Now in contrast to this, I found it very easy indeed to write about the brother I invented. I do have a brother, and I have always got on very well with him. He is not called Bert, like the brother in my poem, and though he used to keep animals in cages in his bedroom, he never kept anything bigger than a hedgehog. And he never went to school with a mouse in his shirt, that I know of. Somebody else did that. Nevertheless, when I came to invent this brother Bert for my poem, I found it easy. He came alive immediately. My feelings about brothers, evidently, are very plentiful and strong and also easy to use. Now if you were to invent some relatives, you might find it the other way round: you might find yourself stuck with the brother but reeling off pages about the mother. Here is the piece about brother Bert:

Pets are the Hobby of my brother Bert,
He used to go to school with a Mouse in his shirt.

His Hobby it grew, as some hobbies will,
And grew and *grew* and GREW until—

Oh don't breathe a word, pretend you haven't heard.
A simply appalling thing has occurred—

The very thought makes me iller and iller:
Bert's brought home a gigantic Gorilla!

If you think that's really not such a scare,
What if it quarrels with his Grizzly Bear?

You still think you could keep your head?
What if the Lion from under the Bed.

And the four Ostriches that deposit
Their football eggs in his bedroom closet

And the Aardvark out of his bottom drawer
All danced out and joined in the Roar?

What if the Pangolins were to caper
Out of their nests behind the wallpaper?

With the fifty sort of Bats
That hang on his hatstand like old hats,

And out of a shoebox the excitable Platypus
Along with the Ocelot or Jungle-Cattypus?

The Wombat, the Dingo, the Gecko, the Grampus—
How they would shake the house with their Rumpus?

Not to forget the Bandicoot
Who would certainly peer from his battered old boot.

Why it could be a dreadful day,
And what Oh what would the neighbours say!

If you are bored by your relatives, it is very amusing to re-invent them. It is a kind of mild revenge on them for being as they are. And one is doing this sort of thing all the time, anyway. Because our relatives are so firmly fixed in our lives, we are always dreaming fantasies around them, whether we know it or not. An uncle of mine was a carpenter, and always making curious little toys and ornaments out of wood. That is the only clue I can find for the origins of this next poem, about Uncle Dan:

My Uncle Dan's an inventor, you may think that's very fine,
You may wish he was your Uncle instead of being mine—
If he wanted he could make a watch that bounces when it drops,
He could make a helicopter out of string and bottle tops
Or any really useful thing you can't get in the shops.

But Uncle Dan has other ideas:
The bottomless glass for ginger beers,
The toothless saw that's safe for the tree,
A special word for a spelling bee
(Like Lionocerangoutangadder),
Or the roll-uppable rubber ladder,
The mystery pie that bites when it's bit—
My Uncle Dan invented it.

My Uncle Dan sits in his den inventing night and day.
His eyes peer from his hair and beard like mice from a load of hay.
And does he make the shoes that will go walks without your feet?
A shrinker to shrink instantly the elephants you meet?
A carver that just carves from the air steaks cooked and ready to eat?

No, no, he has other intentions—
Only perfectly useless inventions:
Glassless windows (they never break),
A medicine to cure the earthquake,
The unspillable screwed-down cup,
The stairs that go neither down nor up,
The door you simply paint on a wall—
Uncle Dan invented them all.

I had several other uncles lined up to write about, besides or instead of this one. One real uncle can supply any amount of imaginary uncles, all different. This same uncle of mine was a strong man. He used to fold six-inch nails over the back of his middle finger. Also, when I was very young, he made me a Noah's Ark. Also, he used to have a number of conjuring tricks. So, with a bit of imagination, here I have several uncles straight off: the world's strongest man, or, perhaps, the great wrestler who was challenged and defeated by a grasshopper. Then there is the uncle who was Noah. Then there is, what my uncle did when the great flood came, and My uncle the Fire-fighter. Then there is the uncle who was a magician but could not get his spells right, and the terrible things that happened as a result. Then there is the uncle who was the world's biggest simpleton. All perfectly good uncles to write a poem about, when I feel like it, and all suggested to me by this one real uncle.

It does not matter if you do not have an uncle. In fact, it is probably much easier. If you have no uncle, your imagination feels a positive need to create one. For instance, I have never known either of my grandfathers. I have often wondered what they must have been like. How would it be, for instance, if one of them had been a trapper of owls:

The truth of the matter, the truth of the matter—
As one who supplies us with hats is a Hatter,
As one who is known for his growls is a Growler—
My grandpa traps owls, yes, my grandpa's an Owler.

Though owls, alas, are quite out of fashion,
Grandpa keeps busy about his profession
And hoards every owl that falls to his traps:
"Someday," he says, "they'll be needed, perhaps."

"Owls are such sages," he says, "I surmise
Listening to owls could make the world wise."
Nightlong his house is shaken with hoots,
And he wakes to owls in his socks and his boots.

Owls, owls, nothing but owls,
The most fantastical of fowls;
White owls from the Arctic, black owls from the Tropic.
Some are far-sighted, others myopic.

There are owls on his picture frames, owls on his chairs,
Owls in dozens ranked on his stairs.
Eyes, eyes, rows of their eyes.
Some are big as collie dogs, some are thumb-size.

Deep into Africa, high into Tibet
He travels with his rubber mouse and wiry owl-net;
The rarest of owls, and the very most suspicious
Will pounce on the mouse and be tangled in the meshes.

"Whatever you could wish to know, an owl will surely know it,"
My grandpa says proudly, "And how does he show it?
Sleeping and thinking and sleeping and thinking—
Letting a horrible hoot out and winking!"

It is fairly easy, of course, to invent a relative out of thin air.
You do not have to search around for hints. I have racked my
brains to find any clue in what I know of my father for the
origin of this next poem. Maybe I got the hint from somebody
else's father. I have no idea where he came from, but here he is:

Some fathers work at the office, others work at the store,
Some operate great cranes and build up skyscrapers galore,
Some work in canning factories counting green peas into cans,
Some drive all night in huge and thundering removal vans.

But mine has the strangest job of the lot.
My Father's the Chief Inspector of—What?
O don't tell the mice, don't tell the moles,
My Father's the Chief Inspector of HOLES.

It's a work of the highest importance because you never know
What's in a hole, what fearful thing is creeping from below.
Perhaps it's a hole to the ocean and will soon gush water in tons,
Or maybe it leads to a vast cave full of gold and skeletons.

Though a hole might seem to have nothing but dirt in,
Somebody's simply got to make certain.
Caves in the mountain, clefts in the wall,
My Father has to inspect them all.

That crack in the road looks harmless. My Father knows it's not.
The world may be breaking into two and starting at that spot.
Or maybe the world is a great egg, and we live on the shell,
And it's just beginning to split and hatch: you simply cannot tell.

If you see a crack, run to the phone, run!
My Father will know just what's to be done.
A rumbling hole, a silent hole,
My Father will soon have it under control.

Keeping a check on all these holes he hurries from morning to
    night.
There might be sounds of marching in one, or an eye shining
    bright.
A tentacle came groping from a hole that belonged to a mouse,
A floor collapsed and Chinamen swarmed up into the house.

A Hole's an unpredictable thing—
Nobody knows what a Hole might bring.
Caves in the mountain, clefts in the wall,
My Father has to inspect them all!

I do not want to leave you thinking there is nothing to write
about but relatives. All these poems are a sort of joke. Poets
write poems to amuse themselves, partly. The best jokes, of
course, are about real things and real people: one does not have
to be fantastic. The final poem is about something which is
both real and fantastic. You will all have heard of the Loch
Ness Monster, and you will all have heard that it is not real.
Some people think it is real, and some people think it is not.
Loch Ness as you know is in Scotland. The monstrous names
in the poem belong to animals which lived on the earth when
the species of which the Loch Ness monster seems to be a

descendant first appeared. In olden times, the monster used to be worshipped as a goddess, and was called Nessa, so it is quite curious that she should still be called Nessie. Here is the poem, Nessie speaking to herself, lamenting that nobody will believe their eyes when they see her.

No, it is not an elephant or any such grasshopper.
It's shaped like a pop bottle with two huge eyes in the stopper.

But vast as a gasometer, unmanageably vast,
With wing-things like a whale for flying under water fast.

It's me, me, me, the Monster of the Loch!
Would God I were a proper kind, a hippopot or croc!

Mislaid by the ages, I gloom here in the dark,
But I should be ruling Scotland from a throne in Regent's Park!

Once I was nobility—Diplodocus ruled the Isles!
Polyptychod came courting with his stunning ten-foot smiles.

Macroplat swore he'd carry me off before I was much older,
All his buddy-boys were by, grinning over his shoulder—

Leptoclid, Cryptocleidus, Triclid and Ichthyosteg—
Upstart Sauropterygs! But I took him down a peg—

I had a long bath in the Loch and waiting till I'd finished
He yawned himself to a fossil and his gang likewise diminished.

But now I can't come up for air without a load of trippers
Yelling "Look at the neck on it, and look at its hedge clippers!

Oh no, that's its mouth." Then I can't decently dive
Without them sighing, "Imagine! If *that* thing were alive!

Why, we'd simply have to decamp, to Canada, and at the double!
It was luckily only a log, or the loch-bed having a bubble.

It was something it was nothing why whatever could it be
The ballooning hideosity we thought we seemed to see?"

Because I am so ugly that it's just incredible!
The biggest bag of Haggis Scotland cannot swallow or sell!

Me, me, me, the Monster of the Loch,
Scotland's ugliest daughter, seven tons of poppycock!

Living here in my black mud bed the life of a snittery newty,
And never a zoologist a-swooning for my beauty.

O where's the bonnie laddie, so bold and so free,
Who'll drum me up to London and proclaim my pedigree?

CHAPTER NINE

Moon Creatures

There is no end to the things that may exist as yet undiscovered, either on the earth or on some other planet like the earth. I forget how many new creatures are discovered every year even on this earth, but it is a surprisingly large number—very minute creatures they are, of course, for the most part.

However, the number and oddity of the creatures which inhabit the earth or the planets, are nothing to those which inhabit our minds, or perhaps I ought to say our dreams, or the worlds from which our dreams emerge, worlds presumably somewhere out beyond the bottom of our minds. Now it is a fact, deny it as you may, that one of the worlds from which our dreams come seems to be very like the moon. Nobody has ever been there except maybe one or two select madmen. We are satisfied that the real moon exists rolling about in the sky, but we have quite as much evidence for the existence of the dream moon, and as this one is somewhere inside our minds it affects us much more closely than the other, and so ought to be much more our concern.

I recently spent some interesting hours, rather as an astronomer might spend interesting hours at his telescope. Only where the astronomer would be studying that moon so easily visible in the sky, I was studying the moon not quite so easily visible at the bottom of our dreams. The astronomer sees volcanoes, deserts and so on, and astronomers in the past have given all these features names, and just in the same way I have named and described some of the things I saw on this other moon. I do not pretend to have seen more than a tiny fraction of what there is to be seen, of course, and I am by no means the first investigator in the field, but here are a few of the oddities I saw which no one else seems to have yet recorded.

First of all, there is the Earth-owl. On this particular moon of which l am speaking there is a great deal of precious metal and mineral deep in the rock, so mining is one of the chief industries—rather like coal-mining on the earth, only much more extensive and thorough. The miners in these moon-mines are often interrupted by a bird called the earth-owl which flies through solid rock. Here is what I learned about this bird. I put it into rhymes to amuse myself. *The Earth Owl.*

> Far undergrounded,
> Moon-miners dumbfounded
> Hear the speed-whistle
> Of this living missile
> As he tears through the strata
> Or splits apart a
> Subterrene Gibraltar,
> His wings do not falter
> At deposits of iron—
> He just screws a new eye on
> The end of his skull
> Which is shaped with great skill
> As a terrible drill
> That revolves on his neck—
> His spine is the spindle,
> His body the handle,
> His wings are the thrust—
> In a gunshot of dust
> Sparks, splinters and all he
> Bursts from the mine-wall,
> Shrieking "Ek, Ek!"
> And crashing straight on
> Is instantly gone.

That is a harmless enough creature, though he can be alarming with his sudden emergences and loud cry. But there are several extremely dangerous species on the moon. Numbers, for instance. On earth, numbers as we know them are fairly harmless passive things. We do not think of numbers as having life at all. They just lie around, like tools, waiting to be used. On the moon, it is otherwise. There, numbers are a truly dangerous menace. Here is what I learned about two or three of the most common species. I call them *Moon Horrors*.

When he has dined, the man-eating tiger leaves certain signs.
But nothing betrays the moon's hideous number nines.
Nobody knows where they sleep off their immense meals.
They strike so fatally nobody knows how one feels.
One-eyed, one-legged, they start out of the ground with such a
        shout
The chosen victim's eyes instantly fall out.
They do not leave so much as a hair but smack their chops
And go off thinner than ever with grotesque hops.

Now the shark will take a snack by shearing off half a swimmer.
Over the moon presides a predator even grimmer.
Descending without warning from the interstellar heavens
Whirling like lathes, arrive the fearful horde of number sevens.
Whatever they touch, whether owl or elephant, poet or scientist,
The wretched victim wilts instantly to a puff of purple mist
And before he can utter a cry or say goodbye to kith and kin
Those thin-gut number sevens have sucked him ravenously in.

Mosquitoes seem dreadful, for they drink at a man as he sleeps.
Night and day over the moon a far craftier horror creeps.
It is hard to know what species of creature you would have to be
To escape the attentions of the moon's horrible number three.
He attacks as a nightmare, and the sleeper dreams he is being
        turned inside out
And sucked dry like an orange, and when he wakes it has all come
        about.
Ever afterwards he is perfectly hollow and dry, while his precious
        insides
Nourish some gross number three wherever that monster now
        resides.

But the thing that specialises in hunting down the great hero
Is the flying strangler, the silent zero.
It is luckily quite rare, perhaps there is only one.
According to legend it lives sleepily coiled around the sun.
But when a moon-hero appears it descends and hovers just over
    his head.
His enemies call it a halo, but his friends see it and tremble with
    dread.
And sure enough, in the very best of his days,
That zero drops around his neck, tightens, and whirls away with
    him into the sun's blaze.

Most things on the moon, I must confess, seem to be peril-
ous in some way. Music there, for one thing, is not at all like
music here. "The sweet power of music", says Shakespeare,
and he implies that breasts too savage to be soothed by music
are not fit for human company. But music on the moon is not
expected to soothe. Here is what I learned about the music of
several familiar instruments in common use there. *Moon
Music*.

The pianos on the moon are so long
The pianist's hand must be fifteen fingers strong.

The violins on the moon are so violent
They have to be sunk in deep wells, and then they only seem to
    be silent.

The bassoons on the moon blow no notes
But huge blue loons that flap slowly away with undulating
    throats.

Now harmonicas on the moon are humorous,
The tunes produce German Measles, but the speckles more
    numerous.

Of a trumpet on the moon you can never hear enough
Because it puffs the trumpeter up like a balloon and he floats off.

Double basses on the moon are a risk all right,
At the first note enormous black hands appear and carry away
    everything in sight.

Even a triangle on the moon is risky,
One ping—and there's your head a half bottle of Irish whisky.

In the same way, be careful with the flute—
Because wherever he is, your father will find himself converted
    into a disgusting old boot.

On the whole it's best to stick to the moon's drums.
Whatever damage they do is so far off in space the news never
    comes.

Some things up there are very like certain things on earth,
but inside out, or upside down, or the other way round. For
instance, they have civil war up there. This is common enough
on earth. A civil war has been going on, somewhere on earth,
at almost any time during the last fifteen years—sometimes
several at the same time. But the rule of civil wars on earth is
to be brief. On the moon, it seems, the civil war will go on at
least as long as the moon does. Here is my account of the
antagonists, their weapons, and their hopes.

Many as the troubles upon the old moon are,
The worst is its unending civil war.

The soldiers of the Moon-Dark are round and small.
Each clanks like a tank, blue armour covering all.
He wears asbestos overalls under his clatter
So if he's thrown to the volcanoes it does not matter.

His weapon is a sackful of bloodsucking vampires
(Wars on the moon are without rules or umpires)
He flings these bats one at a time into the enemy host.
When it returns full he sends it to the first aid post
Where it gives up the blood for transfusions later in the battle,
Then it flies back to its owner with renewed mettle.

The soldiers of the Moon-Light are tall and thin.
They seem to be glisteningly naked, but are in fact silvered with
    tin.
They are defensive fighters, but pretty hot—
Their armament is an electric torch and a lobsterpot.
They flash their beam into the vampire's eyes and so puzzle it,
Then cram the lobsterpot onto its head, and so muzzle it.

They long for the last great battle in which they will catch
Every vampire the Moon-Darkers have been able to hatch.
Then they will rush upon the helpless Moon-Darkers and soon
With knitting needles abolish them forever from the face of the
    moon.

That is a pretty unfamiliar situation except for the fighting.
The snail of the moon, on the other hand, is exactly like the
snail on earth—the common sort of snail. With two important
differences: its voice and its size. Here is the *Snail of the Moon*.

Saddest of all things on the moon is the snail without a shell.
You locate him by his wail, a wail heart-rending and terrible

Which sounds as though some thing had punctured him.
His battle for progress is both slow and grim.

He is sad, wet and cold, like a huge tear
In a thin skin. He wanders far and near

Searching for a shelter from the sun—
For the first sun-beam will melt and make him run.

So moving in moon-dark only he must keep going,
With muscles rippling and saliva flowing,

But nowhere on the moon is there garage
For such a snail. He is not merely large

He is over a mile from side to side.
It's useless him seeking any place to hide.

So wailingly and craning his periscopes
Over the dark bulge of the moon he gropes.

He has searched every inch of the moon. I guess
That silver is snail-saliva silveriness.

It is peculiar how things have got mixed up on the moon.
You would think fox-hunting could simply not be other than
it is on earth. It could, of course, and on the moon it is. On the
moon, the *foxes* have the upper hand, and when they feel like
some jolly exercise they hunt—not foxes but men. Here is the
Moon Man-hunt.

A man-hunt on the moon is full of horrible sights and sounds.
There are these foxes in red jackets, they are their own horses
and hounds.
They have unhuman eyes, O they are savage out of all bounds.

They swagger at the meet, their grins going back under their ears.
They are sociable to begin with, showing each other their long
fangs and their no fears.
They pretend it is all a good game and nothing to do with death
and its introductory tears.

Now one yip! and they are off, tails waving in sinister accord.
To tell the truth, they are a murderous depraved-looking horde.
Sniff sniff! they come over the acres, till some strolling squire
looks up and sees them pattering toward.

The sweat jumps on his brow freezingly and the hair stands on
his thighs.
His lips writhe, his tongue fluffs dry as a duster, tears pour from
his eyes.
His bowels twist like a strong snake, and for some seconds he
sways there useless with terrified surprise.

"Ha Ha!" go all the foxes in unison.
"That menace, that noble rural vermin, the gentry, there's one!"
The dirt flies from their paws and the squire begins hopelessly
to run.

But what chance does that wretch have against such an animal?
Five catch his heels, and one on his nose, and ten on each arm,
    he goes down with a yell.
It is terrible, it is terrible, O it is terrible!

It would seem that the moon copies the earth in lots of things, but is not very good at accurate copies. It makes mistakes. Things that should grow on roots, run on legs, and so on.

There is moon-hops. Hops, as you know, are grown to go into the making of beer. But on the moon it is quite different. They look pretty much the same as on earth, long leafy vine-things, but they do not grow up poles in an orderly fashion. Not at all. There is nothing much to say about them, but I noted down the essentials. *Moon-Hops*.

Hops are a menace on the moon, a nuisance crop.
From hilltop to hilltop they hop hopelessly without stop
Nobody knows what they want to find, they just go on till they
    drop,
Clip-clop at first, then flip-flop, then slip-slop, till finally they
    droopily drop and all their pods pop.

Finally, Foxgloves. I recorded details of quite a few more things than I have mentioned here, but I do not want to strain your credulity too far. Foxgloves on earth, of course, are a rather pretty flower—towers of wild, speckled magenta bells. On the moon, not so. On the moon, as no doubt by now you will expect, foxgloves are perhaps not a flower at all. It is hard to say what they are, they have never been seen. They only leave evidence. And here is how they apparently operate. *Foxgloves*.

Foxgloves on the moon keep to dark caves.
They come out at the dark of the moon only and in waves
Swarm through the moon-towns and wherever there's a chink
Slip into the houses and spill all the money, clink-clink,
And crumple the notes and re-arrange the silver dishes,
And dip hands into the goldfish bowls and stir the goldfishes,
And thumb the edges of mirrors, and touch the sleepers
Then at once vanish into the far distance with a wild laugh
    leaving the house smelling faintly of Virginia Creepers.

Words and Experience

Sitting in a chair is simple enough, and seems to need no commentary. To see an aircraft cross the sky, while a crow flies in the opposite direction, is simple enough, and again we do not feel compelled to remark on it. To read a letter from the other side of the world, and then go and collect the debt it asks us to collect from somebody near, may not be so easy, but it needs no commentary. We do not need to describe to ourselves every step, very carefully, before we are able to take it. Words need not come into it. We imagine the whole situation, and the possible ways of dealing with it, and then proceed in the way that seems best. Our imagination works in scenes, things, little stories and people's feelings. If we imagine what someone will say, in reply to something we intend to say or do, we have first to imagine how they will feel. We are as a rule pretty confident we know how they will feel. We may be terribly wrong, of course, but at least we never doubt that it is what they feel which counts. And we can think like this without ever forming a single word in our heads. Many people, perhaps most of us, do think in words all the time, and keep a perpetual running commentary going or a mental conversation, about everything that comes under our attention or about something in the back of our minds. But it is not essential. And the people who think in dumb pictures and dim sensings seem to manage just as well. Maybe they manage even better. You can imagine who is likely to be getting most out of reading the gospels, for instance: the one who discusses every sentence word by word and argues the contradictions and questions every obscurity and challenges every absurdity, or the one who imagines, if

only for a few seconds, but with the shock of full reality, just what it must have been like to be standing near when the woman touched Christ's garment and he turned round.

It is the same with all our experience of life: the actual substance of it, the material facts of it, embed themselves in us quite a long way from the world of words. It is when we set out to find words for some seemingly quite simple experience that we begin to realize what a huge gap there is between our understanding of what happens around us and inside us, and the words we have at our command to say something about it.

Words are tools, learned late and laboriously and easily forgotten, with which we try to give some part of our experience a more or less permanent shape outside ourselves. They are unnatural, in a way, and far from being ideal for their job. For one thing, a word has its own definite meanings. A word is its own little solar system of meanings. Yet we are wanting it to carry some part of our meaning, of the meaning of our experience, and the meaning of our experience is finally unfathomable, it reaches into our toes and back to before we were born and into the atom, with vague shadows and changing features, and elements that no expression of any kind can take hold of. And this is true of even the simplest experiences.

For instance, with that crow flying across, beneath the aeroplane, which I instanced as a very simple sight—how are we going to give our account of that? Forgetting for a moment the aircraft, the sky, the world beneath, and our own concerns—how are we to say what we see in the crow's flight? It is not enough to say the crow flies purposefully, or heavily, or rowingly, or whatever. There are no words to capture the infinite depth of crowiness in the crow's flight. All we can do is use a word as an indicator, or a whole bunch of words as a general directive. But the ominous thing in the crow's flight, the barefaced, bandit thing, the tattered beggarly gipsy thing, the caressing and shaping yet slightly clumsy gesture of the downstroke, as if the wings were both too heavy and too powerful,

and the headlong sort of merriment, the macabre pantomime ghoulishness and the undertaker sleekness—you could go on for a very long time with phrases of that sort and still have completely missed your instant, glimpse knowledge of the world of the crow's wingbeat. And a bookload of such descriptions is immediately rubbish when you look up and see the crow flying.

Nevertheless, there are more important things than crows to try and say something about. Yet that is an example of how words tend to shut out the simplest things we wish to say. In a way, words are continually trying to displace our experience. And in so far as they are stronger than the raw life of our experience, and full of themselves and all the dictionaries they have digested, they do displace it.

But that is enough for the moment about the wilfulness of words. What about our experience itself, the stuff we are trying to put into words—is that so easy to grasp? It may seem a strange thing to say, but do we ever know what we really do know?

A short time ago, a tramp came to our door and asked for money. I gave him something and watched him walk away. That would seem to be a simple enough experience, watching a tramp walk away. But how could I begin to describe what I saw? As with the crow, words seem suddenly a bit thin. It is not enough to say "The tramp walked away" or even "The tramp went away with a slinking sort of shuffle, as if he wished he were running full speed for the nearest corner". In ordinary descriptive writing such phrases have to suffice, simply because the writer has to economize on time, and if he set down everything that is to be seen in a man's walk he would never get on to the next thing, there would not be room, he would have written a whole biography, that would be the book. And even then, again just as with the crow, he would have missed the most important factor: that what he saw, he saw and understood in one flash, a single 1,000-volt shock, that lit up everything and drove it into his bones, whereas in such words and

phrases he is dribbling it out over pages in tinglings that can only just be felt.

What *do* we see in a person's walk? I have implied that we see everything, the whole biography. I believe this is in some way true. How we manage it, nobody knows. Maybe some instinctive and involuntary mimicry within us reproduces that person at first glance, imitates him so exactly that we feel at once all he feels, all that gives that particular uniqueness to the way he walks or does what he is doing. Maybe there is more to it. But however it works, we get the information.

It is one thing to get the information, and quite another to become conscious of it, to know that we have got it. In our brains there are many mansions, and most of the doors are locked, with the keys inside. Usually, from our first meeting with a person, we get some single main impression, of like or dislike, confidence or distrust, reality or artificiality, or some single, vivid something that we cannot pin down in more than a tentative, vague phrase. That little phrase is like the visible moving fin of a great fish in a dark pool: we can see only the fin: we cannot see the fish, let alone catch or lift it out. Or usually we cannot. Sometimes we can. And some people have a regular gift for it.

I remember reading that the novelist H. E. Bates was in the habit of inventing quick brief biographies or adventures for people he met or saw who struck his imagination. Some of these little fantasies he noted down, to use in his stories. But as time passed, he discovered that these so-called fantasies were occasionally literal and accurate accounts of the lives of those very individuals he had seen. The odd thing about this, is that when he first invented them, he had thought it was all just imagination, that he was making it all up. In other words, he had received somehow or other accurate information, in great detail, by just looking—but hadn't recognized it for what it was. He had simply found it lying there in his mind, at that moment, unlabelled.

The great Swiss psycho-analyst Jung describes something

similar in his autobiography. During a certain conversation, he wanted to illustrate some general point he was trying to make, and so just for an example he invented a fictitious character and set him in a fictitious situation and described his probable actions—all to illustrate his point. The man to whom he was speaking, somebody he had never met before, became terribly upset, and Jung could not understand why, until later, when he learned that the little story he had invented had been in fact a detailed circumstantial account of that man's own private life. Somehow or other, as they talked, Jung had picked it up—but without recognizing it. He had simply found it when he reached into his imagination for any odd materials that would make up a story of the kind he wanted.

Neither of these two men would have realized what they had learned if they had not both had occasion to invent stories on the spot, and if they had not by chance discovered later that what had seemed to them pure imagination had also somehow been fact. Neither had recognized their own experience. Neither had known what they really knew.

There are records of individuals who have the gift to recognize their experience at once, when it is of this sort. At first meeting with a stranger, such people sometimes see his whole life in a few seconds, like a film reeling past, in clear pictures. When this happens, they cannot help it. They simply see it, and know at once that it belongs to this person in front of them. Jung and Bates also saw it, but did not know—and they saw it only in an odd way, when they compelled themselves to produce a story at that very moment. And I believe we all share this sort of reception, this sort of experience, to some degree.

There are other individuals who have the gift to recognize in themselves not simply experience of this sort, but even a similar insight into the past lives and adventures of objects. Such people are known as psychometrists, and have been used by the police. From some weapon or tool used in a crime, they can as it were read off a description of the criminal and often a great deal about him. They are not infallible. But the best of them have amazing records of successes. They take hold of the particular object and the knowledge they are after flashes across their imaginations. Again, it is said by some that this is a gift we all share, potentially, that it is simply one of the characteristics of being alive in these mysterious electrical bodies of ours, and the difficult thing is not to pick up the information but to recognize it—to accept it into our consciousness. But this is not surprising. Most of us find it difficult to know what we are feeling about anything. In any situation, it is almost impossible to know what is really happening to us. This is one of the penalties of being human and having a brain so swarming with interesting suggestions and ideas and self-distrust.

And so with my tramp, I was aware of a strong impression all right, which disturbed me for a long time after he had gone. But what exactly had I learned? And how could I begin to delve into the tangled, rather painful mass of whatever it was that stirred in my mind as I watched him go away.

And watching a tramp go away, even if you have just been subliminally burdened with his entire biography, is a slight experience compared to the events that are developing in us all the time, as our private history and our personal make-up and hour by hour biological changes and our present immediate circumstances and all that we know, in fact, struggle together, trying to make sense of themselves in our single life, trying to work out exactly what is going on in and around us, and exactly what we are or could be, what we ought and ought not to do, and what exactly did happen in those situations which though we lived through them long since still go on inside us as if time could only make things fresher.

And all this is our experience. It is the final facts, as they are registered on this particular human measuring instrument. I have tried to suggest how infinitely beyond our ordinary notions of what we know our real knowledge, the real facts for us, really is. And to live removed from this inner universe of experience is also to live removed from ourself, banished from ourself and our real life. The struggle truly to possess his own experience, in other words to regain his genuine self, has been man's principal occupation, wherever he could find leisure for it, ever since he first grew this enormous surplus of brain. Men have invented religion to do this for others. But to do it for themselves, they have invented art—music, painting, dancing, sculpture, and the activity that includes all these, which is poetry.

Because it is occasionally possible, just for brief moments, to find the words that will unlock the doors of all those many mansions inside the head and express something—perhaps not much, just something—of the crush of information that presses in on us from the way a crow flies over and the way a man walks and the look of a street and from what we did one day a dozen years ago. Words that will express something of the deep complexity that makes us precisely the way we are, from the momentary effect of the barometer to the force that created men distinct from trees. Something of the inaudible music that moves us along in our bodies from moment to moment like water in a river. Something of the spirit of the snowflake in the water of the river. Something of the duplicity and the relativity and the merely fleeting quality of all this. Something of the almighty importance of it and something of the utter meaninglessness. And when words can manage something of this, and manage it in a moment of time, and in that same moment make out of it all the vital signature of a human being—not of an atom, or of a geometrical diagram, or of a heap of lenses—but a human being, we call it poetry.